The Opposite of Socialism

Why our politics is broken

Andrew Galloway

Published by:

Amazon

© 2019 Andrew Galloway

All territories (worldwide rights)

All rights reserved

ISBN 9781099113666

To the brave libertarians who stand up in the face of mighty adversity to defend their beliefs and, by extension, the rights of all individuals everywhere whose rights are being eroded by the relentless march of socialism. There are too many to mention them all, but they can be found writing books, giving talks and posting videos on the Internet, trying to get their message out to the world and to pass the baton to another before their voices are silenced through censorship or their flame is extinguished by more foul means than this.

To all those brave souls, I salute you in the truest tradition of respect for those who have suffered for the freedom and the rights or all.

To everyone who has ever said "our politics is broken" and who want to hear at least one position on why it is broken, how did it get broken, by whom and what can we do about it?

Contents

Why is our politics broken?

I'm sure you've heard the term "Our politics is broken". You may even have said that very same thing a few times yourself. You only have to look around the world at the UK, the USA, Australia, Canada, France, Germany, Italy, Spain, and the list goes on and on and on. At best, the will of the people is being ignored by the duly elected representatives of the people. At worst, it is being deliberately sabotaged by the political elite that claims to know what is best for the people, even though the people are quite capable of making their own decisions.

The question is not whether our politics is broken. If I came to you and said, "my car is broken", you wouldn't just nod sagely as if that meant something to you. No. You would ask why is it broken i.e. what is it that isn't working properly? How did it break? When did it happen? Whose fault was it? What can be done to fix it? How much will it cost? How long will it take? Who's going to do the work?

In the same way, this small book takes off where most other discussions grind to a halt. When someone says, "our politics is broken", that is normally the final nail in the coffin of that conversation. It appears there is nowhere to go after that statement. This book addresses the why? when? how? and who? of our broken politics. It is written in a light, conversational tone that is easy for lay people to understand. The author reduces complex political machinations down to simple and easy to understand explanations. This book is set to change the very face of politics all over the world and to redefine the political landscape of all western democracies by redefining the political spectrum. It is not the definitive word on political history. It is the only word on what to do about our broken politics.

Introduction

I hear many politicians and opinion influencers make the point that our politics is broken. It is stated as a conclusion and to make a point at the end of a discussion. I am using it as a starting point for this discussion. I accept that our politics is broken. My question is "Why is it broken?" When we consider why it is broken, or to put the question in a form that more readily informs our thinking process, "What is it about our politics that isn't working and how did it get that way?" This book explores what has happened to break our politics and proposes a radical re-drawing of the traditional lines between what is considered the differences between the traditional political "left" and "right".

I grew up in a small town in Dorset, England. I went to a good Church of England Primary School and an excellent boys-only grammar school. Considering the grammar school was attended by the sons of admirals, diplomats and foreign princes, I am surprised to look back and discover that politics and all matters related thereto were not on the curriculum. We had some of the best professors in the sciences, some of the best liberal arts and humanities teachers, great sports facilities and a vast array of extra-curricular activities, but nothing to do with politics. Even the debate team, of which I was a sometimes member, did not table motions of a political nature.

Imagine my surprise when, after joining the Royal Navy at the age of nineteen, I found the job I was doing and the training I was receiving were both so closely controlled by politics. Not only because of the policy commitments made by the government of the day and not only political machinations that had created military alliances in the form of NATO, but also in response to political situations from half-way around the world such as the Falklands War in 1982 and the Gulf War in 1987. In 1984 the coal miners' strike affected me by preventing the completion of HMS Edinburgh, which was being built in Cammell Lairds Shipbuilders on Merseyside as the shipbuilders' unions decided to strike in sympathy with the coal miners, thereby ensuring the destruction of their own industry alongside the coal mining industry. In

Introduction

a very real and direct way politics was having an immediate effect on my life on an almost daily basis. I saw up close and personal how decisions made for political expediency or based on deep seated political beliefs can impact the well-being and livelihoods of millions of people, whether they are politically motivated or not.

In 2016, I was deeply concerned with the referendum in Britain that could lead to Britain withdrawing from the EU or becoming ever more enmeshed into the EU political machine. I was around at the time that the UK voted to join the Common Market, as it was then. I was pleased with the result, even though I was not old enough to vote and therefore was not part of the decision-making process. The basic argument for joining was "A bigger market is better". The logic of this simple statement is irrefutable. Would you like to have more customers or not? Would you like to sell more goods or not? Interestingly, the decision to join the Common Market was not about the UK being able to buy more goods from more places or to buy them cheaper. At the time, Britain was still very much associated with the British Commonwealth, a hang-over from the "days of empire" that even today very few countries have opted out of and that contains over a third of the world's population. The British Commonwealth was (and still is) one of the most successful economic unions in history, The UK had access to a vast selection of goods and services from all over the world in mutually beneficial, not highly regulated, trade arrangements. Commonwealth citizens were able to travel and work all around the world with very little bureaucracy and very few restrictions.

Fast forward to 2016, to a time when the EU had taken over from the Common Market, promising ever closer political union, it had just announced its plans for a European Army, the Euro was failing to the extent that most of the Mediterranean countries were either bankrupt or getting very close and Germany's Chancellor is hinting at plans to ensure Deutschemarks could be printed again, doubtless and in my opinion, in expectation of the Euro failing completely in the very near future. The government in the UK announced a referendum will be held to determine whether to remain in the EU or to leave the EU. In the USA, Donald Trump had just been elected as the 45th president of the United States, flying in the face of the deep-seated political machine that was used to having all the control. In France,

The Opposite of Socialism

Emmanuel Macron had to pull out some very underhand tactics to stop the rise of the populist Marion Anne Perrine "Marine" Le Pen. Without Macron rallying all opposition parties under one flag, many of those parties destroying their own manifestos and their own credibility in the process, Marine Le Pen would have won the election, ushering in a populist era in France, the very birthplace of populism in the form of Egalité.

It was against this backdrop that I became interested in politics in a serious way for the first time in my life at the age of 56. I saw conflict and confusion everywhere I looked. I saw political games being played and I saw a massive rift appear before what is popularly referred to as the "left" and the "right" of politics. I also saw a lot of misunderstanding of those terms and how they were applied to different people and different groups, very often to disparage anyone with a different political view.

What did I observe that made me want to write this book? The political world was one of polarity. Politics in western society[1] was not working. Everyone was talking, no-one was listening. Everyone believed that their way of looking at the world was right and everyone else was wrong. There was no room for compromise or middle ground. I also observed that there is no opposition to socialist policies. Even when a conservative government is in power, socialist policies abound, a legacy of an earlier administration. It was also baffling to those people that thought about it that there is no money, everyone is in debt. As national debt spirals out of control, we cannot afford the socialist programmes that were put in place in better times.

This was the start point of my research about why there is so much confusion about the left and the right, the battle apparently between socialism and capitalism. I researched the towering figure whose followers and advocates credit with putting everything into perspective. I am talking about Karl Marx, founder of Socialism in its many forms, and the author of many writings about the evil of capitalism and the

---

[1] In this book, the term "Western Societies" is a shorthand that refers to cultures based on Judeo Christian values, which have shaped societies predominantly throughout Europe and from there, the rest of the world as the European nations expanded via colonialism. A western society is generally some form of representative democracy and contains some socialist values but a healthy dollop of capitalism also.

Introduction

virtues of the collective. It was two years later that I discovered that this is from where the fundamental rift in modern politics stems. Followers of Karl Marx have made a fundamental assumption based on his writings that has led them down the wrong path ever since. Opponents of Socialism have responded to this incorrect paradigm, causing them to also miss the mark.

This book is my attempt to bring clarity to a very confused society, hopefully before it tears itself apart in its own hated and self-loathing. It may sound grandiose, but I hope this book will be instrumental in enlightening our political classes and our politically aware citizens and lead to more harmony and better decisions that benefit everyone in our societies. As a starting point, the whole political landscape will need to be redefined.

Andy Galloway

Southampton, UK

January 2019

Chapter 1

The History of Politics

There has always been politics in the dealings between one human being and another. The politics evolve naturally to ensure the survival of the species. We can assume the politics of the earliest groups of humans based on the politics that we see in other groups of animals.

Tribalism

This may not be what actually happened as groups of humans started to build their primal societies, but we will never know and, it really doesn't matter that much. What we do know is that under certain circumstances, humans revert to tribalism very easily. Tribalism presented itself as a loyalty to "The Group" over all other groups. This tendency predominantly protected the group from natural disasters, predators and other groups of humans. Survival of The Group depended upon a number of strategies and a number of social constructs being implemented. All successful human groups have adopted similar arrangements. We can only surmise that other groups who were not disposed to Tribalism were unsuccessful. This would indicate that Tribalism is built into the race memory and the DNA of all of us that descended from those tribes that survived.

Success strategies for the tribe involve hunting for meat, gathering of other foods, safe procreation, protection for the young, teaching and training for the youth so that they can take their place as a useful member of the tribe and protection of the whole tribe. These are fundamental to the success of the tribe. However, sometimes these strategies require the sacrifice, whether wilful or otherwise, of some of the individuals that make up the tribe. For example, hunting or war may result in the deaths of a few individuals. But as long as the birth rate was greater than the death rate, the tribe could survive. Many tasks became specialized. For example, hunting was not a skill that came naturally to most people. They had to be able to make and use weapons, they would be fit and strong, preferably a fast runner and they would have to be able to work as part of a team. The up side is that they would generally have the choice of mates as they would have prestige within the tribe and, if there was a shortage of food the hunters would rarely be the ones to go without. The hunters get the lion's share of everything to keep them strong and loyal to The Group, because they were the tribe's best chance of overcoming the food shortage. Similarly, if the tribe was under threat from another group, the warriors would need to be in peak physical shape to stave off the threat and their loyalty to The Group would need to be absolute. If the warriors were given the scraps and left overs and were not allowed to procreate with a mate of their choice, their loyalty could not be guaranteed, and probably should not be expected, if there was a better offer on the table. In early tribes, the hunters and the warriors were one and the same. There is a predisposition for the strongest or most ruthless person in the tribe to rise to the position of leader or Tribal Chief. They are not generally the best suited for the position, but no-one else in the tribe can oust them without putting their own life in danger.

Many of these specialized tasks rely on the acquisition of knowledge, normally by an individual. Expertise in tasks increased the tribe's chances of survival. This may be the best way to harvest and store fruits, to the migratory patterns of certain animals, developing the best weapons, or strategies for winning a war against a similar sized army. In many of these situations, success equals survival and failure equals obliteration. Soon, the individuals that held this knowledge became invaluable to the tribe not for what they could do, but for what they knew. When each member of the tribe was valued only for what they could contribute in terms of actual labour, as soon as their labour was withdrawn through injury, disease or failing health with age, the tribe would no longer allow that member to benefit from the tribe's collective efforts. In times of plenty, the frail and injured would find scraps and left overs that could sustain them. As soon as there is a shortage of food, the frail and injured would die. In war, the sick and the slow are the first ones to fall.

This new-found reliance on expertise marked the end of the "survival by luck" for the tribe and ushered in a new era of "survival by planning". A social engineer could plan and make sure that the tribe had enough hunters, warriors and gatherers. They could ensure that the youth would be taught effectively the skills on which the tribe would later rely and that there were enough of them. The person that holds this knowledge is often the adviser to the Chief. In many cases this person would become the Chief's mate and they would rule the tribe with intelligence when possible and with ruthlessness when required.

This was an incredibly successful political formula that allowed the human race to grow from a handful of savages wandering the plains of Africa to many thousands of people spread to all areas where survival was reasonable easy. This chapter in the evolution of the human society was a success by any standard of measurement.

Feudalism

The success of Tribalism led to Feudalism. The tribal Chief took on the responsibility for all of the decisions that affect the tribe, whether that matter was internal within the tribe or external i.e. dealing with other tribes. This marks the birth of politics proper. The Chief would have specialized advisers for matters to do with running of the tribe and all internal matters related thereto. He would also have specialized advisers to advise on external matters such as war, peace and trade with other tribes. This also led to the rise of diplomacy and the stationing of personnel within the territories of another tribe in an ambassadorial capacity, a direct line of communication between two feudal leaders, simplifying diplomacy and reducing errors caused by miscommunication.

The tribal Chief in a Feudal system will be the royalty. Kings and queens give rise to princes and princesses and rules are established for succession to the throne. Minor royalty such as barons and earls would be given jurisdiction over an area of land and the people that live there. Some of these people would be serfs, owned by and working for the local Lord of the Manor. They tend the lord's animals, fields and rivers. In return, they are allowed to keep part of the crop that they produce for their own families. Families that live and work within the lord's household get fed as servants. Other people would be peasants. They are free people and they work the lord's land in return for wages or the right to sell part of the produce that they create.

The Opposite of Socialism

Peasants wanting to sell part of their produce or exchange it for someone else's goods gives rise to trading, which gives rise to merchants. Merchants are specialized at matching produce with the prospective buyer. Merchants can conspire to ensure an acceptable quality of goods are exchanged for an acceptable amount of money. The merchant would keep a small percentage of the profit or the goods for payment for his services. In turn, this became a skill and those that acquired the skill and expertise were soon catapulted into the higher echelons in terms of wealth creating. Many times, throughout history, merchants have been worth much more than the local king, often to their detriment. One prominent example is the massacre and disbanding of the Templar Knights by the King of France, who was trying to seize all of their wealth, unsuccessfully I might add.

In general terms, Feudalism has a ruling class and a working class. The ruling class offers protection, food, shelter and safety to the working class. In turn, the working class provide the wealth and material support to the ruling class, even to the point of supplying fighting men for the king's battles. In local conflicts, this also allows the working class to join the effort to ensure they are protected. The ruling class has complete dominion over the working class.

Rules were developed to ensure the smooth working of all of the business of state, dealing with foreign and domestic merchants and control of citizens at home. It was determined that if a king gave safe passage to the merchants of another king, then in turn his own merchants were safer in their travels. If a minor lord with a bad temper killed his serfs without any real reason, it would adversely affect his standard of living and make other serfs far more likely to lose their loyalty towards him. Ruling in fear only works moderately well and never for a very long period of time. Such a feudal system is referred to as a Dictatorship. All dictatorships are transitory and cannot last. However, they have been known to kill hundreds of millions of their own subjects before their inevitable collapse.

Feudalism was, and still is in many parts of the world, an incredibly successful political formula that allowed the human race to grow from several thousands of people to many millions of people, who spread to all parts of the globe where survival could be at least made bearable by the use of human ingenuity and the will to shape their environment. Tool making, construction, weapons manufacture, agriculture, language and politics all flourished during this period.

Capitalism

Capitalism is not really a political system. However, it is necessary to consider it as such because of the place it took in the history of politics. It was capitalism that caused Karl Marx to ponder over the economic state of Europe in the mid-1800s. His perception of capitalism was one of exploitation of the workers, predominantly by the merchant class.

Prior to this time, the merchant class were often the wealthiest citizens in any society. Therefore, it stands to reason that if someone wants to buy a property or start a business, they should go to a local merchant to borrow the money and hopefully, gain some insights into how to be successful at their venture. In turn, the merchant would lend the money for a fixed increase in the amount of the loan, referred to as "usury" and today called "interest". Often the merchant would lay claim to part of the business venture as well as charging for the loan. In the case of a person wishing to set themselves up as a merchant, they may determine that they need a ship and a crew and some money to buy goods to transport out and to buy goods for the return journey. Some ventures may involve as many as twenty investors, each investor only taking 5% of the risk but only getting 5% of the reward. This was seen to be a good practice because a certain number of ships sent out didn't return. A class of merchant arose where they would insure such ventures for a fixed fee, without taking a share of the venture themselves.

Many merchants wanted to be able to keep their money safe. Very often they would rent space in the vaults of the local king, which was not always wise as it was the king that was the greatest threat to their money. Instead, someone built a secure facility, a "bank", to store merchant's gold and would charge a small fee for the protection offered. The banker would issue a receipt to their client for the amount of gold on deposit at the bank. Because gold was unnecessarily burdensome, and locked in a vault, it became common practice to exchange these bank receipts or bank notes instead of withdrawing the gold to pay a debt and then the new owner of the gold deposit the gold back in the bank. It was far easier to just exchange the bank notes. Usage and utility then dictated smaller and more useful denominations of bank note be produced. Very small denominations were in the form of metal coins that had the same face value as the inherent value of the metal contained in them.

The banker soon realized that they had at their disposal a tremendous asset in the form of "other people's money" that they could use and make even more money from, with no expense and at no risk to themselves. The banker would lend a small proportion of the money from their vault to other, worthwhile and reasonably safe investors. The fact that the money belonged to someone else didn't deter the bankers from lending the money at their disposal and charging usury to the borrower. Anyway, the gold stayed safely in the vault while the banker simply wrote additional bank notes to cover these additional loans. The bank would only have been in trouble if all of their clients wanted their money at the same time. As long as the bank only lent a proportion of the money in its vaults, retaining enough to cover any expected withdrawals by the clients, no one would be any the wiser.

Because of the advent of the banking system, capitalism developed. Capitalism was once described as the art of staying at home and sending your money out to work for you. Capitalism is a wealth generating system. As I stated earlier, it is not a political system. However, the political implication of capitalism is that it drove the rich to become richer and the poor to become poorer. This has led to massive wealth inequality over the years to the point that in 2019, 90% of the wealth of the world is in the hands of 1% of the population. If people are not looking very carefully, they perceive that wealth inequality is responsible for many of the problems in our society. This is a red herring and keeps our eyes from the truth of the matter.

Socialism

However, it was this inequality of wealth that started to make a significant impact on society in the 18th century that interested Karl Marx. Karl Marx postulated that these inequalities will lead to social unrest, which in turn will lead to a massive uprising of the proletariat (the workers) in Europe in the mid-20th Century. It has perplexed many of his followers why that did not happen. At last we know the answer. In his writings, he expounds the virtues of a political system that will combat the inequalities of capitalism. He termed the phrase "Socialism" to explain a society that is run by and for the benefit of the working class, the proletariat. In his vision of utopia there would be no ruling class. The means of production would belong to the workers and all workers would share in the resultant spoils.

The system proposed by Marx became known as "Marxism" and is often used as a shorthand for Socialism. Socialism seemed to preach the overthrow of the ruling class. This became a very popular idea, even among those that didn't understand the profound implications of its widespread adoption across a society. The reasoning is that we take the excessive amounts of money that the rich has, share it among everyone else then we will all be rich. At the very least, we would all be the same. That sounds fair.

Shortly after his death, the teachings of Karl Marx were adopted by the intelligentsia across Europe. Marxism was then taught to students before they went out into the big, wide world. This accounts for the rise of Marxism and Marxist doctrines so very rapidly in the late 19th century. Marxism was adopted in different countries in the early 20th century. It seems that each country made changes to the doctrine to suit the whims of the local tribal leader, which is as ironic as it sounds.

Socialism quickly fragmented into Communism, Nazi-ism, Fascism, McCarthy-ism, Stalinism, Mao-ism and a whole host of other variations on the socialist theme. What was conspicuous by its absence was any sort of political system that opposed Socialism. Because anti-capitalism was the original message driving the development of Marx's work, everyone just assumed that Capitalism was the opposite of Socialism, that Socialism was created to destroy Capitalism. That is just not the truth of the matter.

Capitalism is a tool that arose from the fact that wealth had been created and the owners of that wealth wanted their money to create more money for them. Thanks to the banking system, there was a way for that to happen. People borrowing some of that money to carry out a worthwhile venture, if that venture were successful, could begin to elevate themselves into the merchant class who could in turn generate wealth for their own use. Capitalism did not dictate who was able to borrow the money to try to become financially successful. Intelligent bankers

The Opposite of Socialism

realized that if they did not back a worthwhile venture, their competitors would. Capitalism was a fair and even-handed system where anyone could start with nothing and become as unequal as they were prepared to work for. The idea that Capitalism is oppressing anyone is expounded by Socialists who don't understand who they are opposing. It must be the rich that are the enemy, even though there is literally nothing stopping anyone who wants to from becoming rich. This is not the definition of exploitation. If it were the enemy, why did none of the Socialist regimes that plagued the planet throughout the 20th Century and so far into the 21st abolish their capitalist system. They didn't. They simply took over ownership of it by the State, State owned capitalism is still capitalism. Even the most ardent Marxists understand that in order to run a society effectively, that society must be able to sell its excess production and purchase things that it cannot or doesn't want to produce. No, Capitalism is not the opposite of Socialism. It is not its enemy and it is not threatened by it.

One of the basic tenets of Socialism is the idea of governing by group identity. It seemed expeditious to write a set of rules for a society that addressed the particular groups within that society. These would be rules like if you are a man between the ages of 18 and 30 you must serve 2 years in the army. Or, if you are of this particular group you are not allowed to own property. The rules had to be written in this manner because those discriminated against by those rules didn't like it and so, the rules had to be policed. One of the basic ideas of police work is that you need to be able to identify when rules are being broken.

The injustice of too many rules meant that many individuals within certain groups were discriminated against over and over again. For example, certain groups may not be allowed to marry, other groups might not hold property, other groups might be barred from borrowing money and yet other groups might not be allowed to walk in public parks. It would be possible and a little unfortunate to belong to all of these groups. In extreme instances, everything that makes life worth living for a person could be stripped away by a socialist regime of group identity politics. But each of the rules in question were passed to make life better for the majority - "for the greater good".

The History of Politics

For centuries, philosophers and science fiction writers alike have concerned themselves with the sheer lunacy of following a set of rules to the nth degree. No one set of rules should be applied in all circumstances, slavishly, to the detriment of many of the people those rules were meant to benefit. For example, suppose that for national security, a curfew has been imposed. Everyone must be home by 6pm. If that is the law of the land, the vast majority of citizens will obey that law. But what if someone has had an emergency and their elderly relative needed a bit more help than could be administered within the allotted time and still allow the carer to get to their own home before the start of the curfew? What then? In most regimes, where soldiers are not allowed to think for themselves, the carer on their way home at 6:30pm would be criminalized, arrested, probably beaten and possibly executed. This based on rules that were meant to protect citizens. Do not worry, by the time you get to the end of this book, you will see that there is light at the end of the tunnel.

Chapter 2

What is the Problem?

There is a deep-seated problem within each and every one of us. Some psychologists refer to it as the duality of human nature. The duality of human nature is a set of values, instincts, feelings, etc. that conspire to do two things, one is to help the individual to survive and the other is to help the species survive. These values change through a person's life and based on changing circumstances. Sometimes individual survival is stronger than the group survival, at other times these roles are reversed. For much of life, these two are mutually compatible and survival of the species is not threatened by the survival of the individual, in fact, in most cases it is enhanced by it. A larger and stronger tribe offers more guarantee of survival for all individuals and therefore the species.

The individual is linked to the group in a fundamental and intrinsic way. Success of the individual very often leads to success of the group. However, the opposite is not necessarily true. This is the fundamental problem at the heart of the duality of human nature. This is what has given rise to politics over the millennia of human domination of Earth. This is the problem that got confuscated by Karl Marx and his drive to continue group identity politics, a drive that has continued to divide us for the last 160 years. The rationale was that the poor workers were being exploited by the rich capitalist owners. Whilst this may have been true in some cases, this was not the root of the problem. There is a story based in the early 19th Century about two American shoe-manufacturing companies that wanted to expand their businesses. They both sent representatives to the South Seas Islands. After several weeks, one reported back to head office "It's a waste of time. No one here wears shoes". The other company representative reported back "Let's get things started. We need a factory and several warehouses out here. No one here wears shoes yet". Using a similar logic, Karl Marx determined that the reason there are so many hard-working people that are poor, yet all of the capitalists are rich must be because the

The Opposite of Socialism

rich are exploiting the poor. Whilst this sounded reasonable, it is not true. It was not true then and it's not true now. The reason there are so many poor people is because of human nature. People equate the rich capitalist with the old tribal chieftain or the lord of the manor, where the man at the top is only able to eat because there are so many people contributing their efforts to keeping him fed. Again, this is a distortion of the truth. The wonder is not that you have rich people. The wonder is that you have poor people, even though the poorest in a western society live better than the wealthy did a few hundred years ago within their equivalent societies. We are all born equal and in any given society, we all have the same equality of opportunity. What this means is that we are free to rise (or fall) to the level of our own contentment. And if we rise to the level of our own contentment, why would we resent others or feel pity for others who have risen to a different level of their own contentment? Did we exploit someone along the way? Or were we exploited somehow? No. We just aimed at and achieved a different level of "success".

Karl Marx would have you believe that people in a "better" position in society, according to his own rules of what is good for you or otherwise, must have exploited you along the way. Karl Marx believed in equality of outcome. Equality of outcome is the fundamental tenet upon which socialism is based. It doesn't matter who you are, what you have done, how hard you have worked or what your current circumstances are, everyone should get an equal share of the pie. This is a dangerous doctrine and it should be rejected out of hand by all intelligent people everywhere and at all times throughout all of history. It doesn't bring the poor up to the level of the rich, it delivers everyone (except the ruling elite) into poverty. If you want to see the results of this policy, you need to look no further than the Russian experiment where 100 million people died in the gulags, Cambodia where 60% of the population were declared dissidents and massacred, Mao's China where 140 million were murdered because they were not committed enough to the cause. Wherever "pure socialism" has been tried, it has led to mass murder, poverty, starvation and social collapse. All in the name of "the greater good". Often and mistakenly, this is referred to as Fascism. It is not, it is Totalitarianism and we will

What is the Problem?

deal with Fascism a bit later. In fact, it is not possible to have a totalitarian state without it being firmly rooted in Socialism.

Here is a very serious question for you to consider. The way you approach this question and the answer that you give will determine your achievements for the rest of your life. Skip to the next paragraph if you are not prepared to face the reality of your own human nature and have it revealed to you in all its unbridled starkness. Ok. You had your chance. The question is that if you lived in a time in history when you were released from the need to hunt and gather your own food, you had access to shelter, medicine and health care, you were largely safe from predators, wars, pestilence and plague, you had the ability to earn as much money as you want, you have access to gadgets and gizmos that can make your work more productive and entertain you, you have the ability to provide education, training and security to your offspring, given all that, what would you do that you're not already doing? That is the question. The reality is that you are living in a Golden Age that mankind has fought and died for and worked towards for all of its time on this planet. What are you doing with this great opportunity and this great abundance? To answer that question is very simple. What did you do yesterday? What did you do the day before? Your future is totally predictable - it is written in your daily routine. Whatever your priorities were yesterday, they are going to be the same today, tomorrow and the next day, until either something changes your priorities, or you die.

"If you want to change some things in your life, then you need to change some things in your life"

Kevin Trudeau

Society is made up of individuals. When the majority of individuals succeed, society succeeds. When the majority of individuals fail, then that society is due to fail. Every single society that has ever existed has ended in ruin, often just after achieving a period of "perfection" or a pinnacle of success. We too are doomed to repeat this pattern if we don't learn from past mistakes and take steps to avoid them. We can learn and continue to grow or we can fail to learn and fall back into barbarism and usher in a new "dark ages". We have the choice, but at the moment we are asking the wrong questions based on an incorrect paradigm.

An individual's job is to succeed, and society's job is to help them do that. Success means different things to different people. Napoleon Hill, author of the towering giant self-help book "Think and Grow Rich" defines success as "the progressive realization of a worthwhile objective". Therefore, if you set out deliberately to become a teacher and you put your heart and soul into being the best teacher you can be and you have a positive impact on the education of a significant number of your students, then you are a success. I'm sure everyone can see how that type of successful teacher can have a positive and beneficial impact on a society. However, the opposite is true. If someone is only a teacher because they couldn't get into law school, their teaching plans are produced at the last minute, classes are delivered in a very lack-lustre way and success of the students is a sometimes thing that is "up to the student", that teacher is not a success. They are just waiting out their lives to retire with a pension, to have a little fun before they die. It is easy to see how that type of teacher can have a negative impact on a society. Success is determined by the individual, measured by their standards, not anyone else's and no one has the right to judge them or tell them where they are wrong or could have done better. So many people would be so much happier if they stopped judging others by their own standards and instead saw the world through the other person's eyes.

Because politics is a macroverse of our dealings with others, there is a duality to the human condition that shows up in our politics, the balance between the good of the group and the welfare of the individual. This balance changes in our politics just as it changes in our individual lives. The balance of our politics can be affected by the results of previous political actions. For example, certain political actions lead to war and as a result politics dictates food rationing, changes in manufacturing focus, conscription of soldiers, etc.

Because the popular misconception of socialism is that it must combat the evils of capitalism and because that basic assertion is incorrect, socialism has always failed to hit its mark i.e. social cohesion. In fact, because socialism does not take full account of its opposite force within the human condition, it is always doomed to failure and failure of socialism always results in human misery. The opposite of socialism is individualism. The driving forces within each of us and therefore within our politics is the need to look after the group and the need to look after the individual. Herein lies the fundamental flaw with modern politics and, insofar as it is reflective of our society, the fundamental cause of the rift in our society.

> *"Socialists don't hate Capitalism, they hate Capitalists"*
> *Andy Galloway*

All individuals want their society to be strong, be safe, have more peace and less war. Individualists want that because it means they and their families have the individual liberty to pursue happiness in whatever form they feel is appropriate for them. If there is peace, they won't be conscripted as cannon fodder for a war effort they don't fundamentally believe in. Individualists believe the way to achieve this utopia is to empower individuals and disempower groups that impose their will on the individual. A great example of a document that enshrines these beliefs is the American Constitution (or the Constitution, if you are reading this in America). This would lead to smaller government that has less rules and regulations and is less intrusive into people's lives. The basic tenet is that you have the sovereign right to pursue happiness on your terms and, as long as you don't infringe on anyone else's rights, you should be left alone to wallow in your happiness. You have the right to defend yourself and your family. However, the government is responsible for ensuring that you are kept safe from dangers that are beyond your ability to combat and to use wisely the money it takes from you. If there are wars, it will be in defence of the way of life of the individuals, something we can all get behind if ever diplomacy fails.

Socialists want the same result, a society that is strong and safe. Unfortunately, they believe the way to achieve that is with a strong and powerful government. Socialists

The Opposite of Socialism

see individuals (well, individuals that have a different belief system from theirs) as the enemy and that enemy must be hemmed in and controlled by regulations and by violent means if necessary. This leads to larger and more powerful government that soaks up more and more money. Because individuals are the enemy, this leads to secrets and clandestine operations that cannot be revealed to the citizens that are paying for the programmes and who are purportedly the beneficiaries of these programmes but who often find themselves the victims just to protect the state from exposure. It is just one short step from there to a dictatorship. In a society where the public leadership must change hands on a regular basis, say every 4 or 8 years, the dictators work behind the throne, in secret, where it does not matter who the public face of the government is or which branch we are considering, the dictators still have the control. We have seen this at play in many countries around the world in the 20th and 21st Century. Often this is referred to as "The Deep State" or "The Permanent Government".

Only socialism can lead to the formation of a Dictatorship or a Deep State scenario. The reason is the inability of socialism to separate the needs of the individual from the needs of the group at a policy level. Socialists believe that anything that empowers the social group is good and anything that weakens the social group is bad. Then they make the link between the needs of the social group and the Government or the State. This is another fundamental flaw. In this case, the State has ceased to be a servant of the people. Whether you consider the citizenry as individuals or as members of various groups is irrelevant to this point. The State is not one of the groups of citizens. It is a machine that should be serving the citizens, not the citizens serving the State. Alarm bells should sound when the state considers itself to be part of the society. That is like saying that a zookeeper is part of the zoo. No. They are necessary to the safe functioning of the zoo, but children go to the zoo to see the animals. Imagine a scenario where the animals were being slaughtered to feed the zookeepers. This would be an absolute travesty of what zookeepers are for and it would begin to destroy the fundamental principles of what the zoo is for in the first place. Imagine then zookeepers have a Zookeepers Intelligence Agency whose job it was to prevent the public from finding out about the animals being used to feed the zookeepers. Imagine what other abuses could be conceived of and undertaken, knowing that the ZIA will prevent anyone from finding out. Now, imagine a new zookeeper who is shocked at learning this truth and who wants to "blow the whistle". What might his fate be? Luckily, this is only conjecture.

"Only Socialism can lead to a dictatorship or a totalitarian state"

Andy Galloway

One of the great inventions of socialism is group identity politics. Placing someone in a group and giving them a label, dehumanizes the individual. It means that people can be treated, not as they need or want, but according to the perceived needs of that group. Often the people who perceive the need of the group do not belong to that group themselves. Another outcome of giving everyone a label is that there is no further need for discussion. It's a bit like the joke where everyone has been in prison for so long that the inmates don't bother telling jokes anymore, they just stand up and shout the number of the joke that they want to tell. Everyone knows to which joke the number refers, so they all laugh. In the same way, in a discussion about immigration, if a socialist doesn't like what the other person is saying, they just shout "racist" or "homophobe" or "Nazi" and it's the end of the discussion. It is pointless trying to continue the rational discussion after that point. This childish naysaying and ad hominem attack also bars meaningful discussions about very real issues of concern to many people.

Individualism doesn't mean not belonging to a group. It means that you chose the groups with which you want to be identified, you don't let others tell you what group you should be in. You don't automatically acquire privilege or a status i.e. victimhood, just for belonging to that group. Socialists like to determine on behalf of everyone, who should belong to which group, what their level of privilege is and what status they have. Everyone must automatically acquire the traits, characteristics and privileges of that group. To do otherwise would get them labelled

The Opposite of Socialism

as "Uncle Tom types", "traitors" "puppets", "racists", or whatever is considered the most hurtful, childish insult.

Group identity politics provides a shorthand for avoiding reasoned argument and intelligent debate. If communication breaks down, progress breaks down. This is the largest contributing factor that causes our politics and our societies to be deeply divided, often over fairly trivial matters. It is rarely observed that an individualist adopts the same tactics because individualists see people as people and not as groups. Therefore, it is very difficult for an individualist to be a racist, a homophobe, a bigot, a sexist etc. because these labels only have any use if you are seeing the world through the lens of identity politics, which is a socialist construct.

So, if Capitalism isn't the opposite of Socialism, what is it? Capitalism, as stated previously, is simply the ability to have your money go out to work for you while you do something else with your time and energy. Any individual can join the capitalist society any time they want. All they need to do is buy shares in a company and they are a capitalist. The problem with capitalism is not what the individual does with it, but how it fits into socialist policies. Before we get into that, let's consider the components of a socialist society as compared to an individualist society.

Both ideologies believe that there must be a "State". The "State" is run by the "Government" of the day, unless you have a Deep State situation, which we will consider later. Often people confuse the State with the Government. In many situations we can use the words interchangeably. To avoid confusion, we should try to use the correct term wherever possible.

The Government is the people that carry out the legislative and executive functions within a society. They do this internally and externally. In internal affairs, it is enough that certain promises were made in a manifesto. Once in power, the promises made in that manifesto are acted upon and legislation is passed and implemented to try to fulfil the manifesto promises. In the case of external matters, there is the additional step of negotiation with other parties before proposing legislation. This negotiation is called diplomacy. If diplomacy is effective and agreement is reached, certain legislation is proposed. If diplomacy fails, then the proposed legislation may be quite different.

What is the Problem?

Once legislation has been passed, the process enters a "set up" phase, if the machinery to implement the legislation does not yet exist. This is a function of Government. However, once the machinery is set up and running, this becomes the domain of The State. The State is the clockwork machinery that has been put in place by Government in the past. It continues under its own cognizance, improving the effectiveness of the machinery but always within the constraints of the legislation that created it in the first place. Government then has an oversight role to ensure that changes made internally, and the production of the end results are what was expected. This is done particularly with a view to providing the stated services within the stated budget. In a healthy society, the Government is answerable to the people and the State is answerable to the Government.

The State is responsible for raising revenues from the people in the form of taxation. That money is then spent on many things, but predominantly the business of both Government and State. Even where money is not ultimately destined to end up in the Government's coffers, such as international relief, it is administered by either Government or State employees. That is why we can use the word state and government completely interchangeably in this book. For purposes of this book, they are the same organization.

Where does the government fit into a socialist society? To answer this, you have to first understand the driving principle of Socialism. It is defined as "a political and economic theory of social organization which advocates that the means of production, distribution, and exchange should be owned or regulated by the community as a whole." In true socialist society there is no need for a State. In fact, when Karl Marx was writing the Communist Manifesto, he envisaged that there were two ways to instal socialism. The first was by revolution, "revolutionary socialism", which holds that socialism can be brought about only by the overthrow of the existing political and societal structures. The other main proponent is "evolutionary socialism", which is basically the idea of getting voters to instal a government that will implement a socialist regime. Both of these ideologies miss the fundamental tenet of socialism. The proletariat should own and be in control of the means of production and exchange. Maintaining or creating a state to take on an elite role within a society is anti-socialist. It makes a mockery of everything Marx believed in.

Where socialist regimes have gone wrong in the past and will continue to go wrong in the future is that they cannot envisage any other way to develop a socialist society except taking over the state and then, using the state to drive the socialist agenda. This is where they get stuck. They take over the state and, for many and varied reasons, some selfish some altruistic, they can't bring themselves to abolish the state and to bring about true socialism. The drivers of this socialist experiment become the new government, the new state, the new elite, the new bourgeoisie. Organized in a very different way and for very different reasons from the old regime, but the new government has a firm belief that what they are doing is for the good of the people that they want to benefit, either themselves or society as a whole. Other people have other ideas and the newly formed quasi-socialist government must guard against any new ideas vigorously. After all, under their benevolent oversight, the society is already on the optimal path to achieve its objectives. So, we don't want anyone rocking the boat, do we? This then leads to new power structures being put in place, secret police, brown-shirts, clandestine courts, gulags and secret prisons. Political opponents disappear in the night. Dissidents accidentally commit suicide. In the case of some socialist leaders, the suspected dissidents were members of their own family (all of them) and in other regimes you could spot a dissident because they wore spectacles or had a modest level of schooling.

So, in a socialist society, Government is seen as the pinnacle of the society, the driving force. Whatever government decrees, the people must do, slavishly and without thinking. Government is the controlling force that holds society together. Socialists drive for a larger and larger state, forgetting the fact that socialism is meant to be abolishing the state altogether.

As the quasi-socialist state continues to grow, because it has an inherent agenda to expand socialism to the rest of the world, it tries to align itself with the states of other countries. This is done through some commonality of trade, intelligence sharing, financial regulations, etc. This then leads to globalist policies, which are still further removed from the individuals. At least there is no pretence at this stage that

What is the Problem?

it is all for the greater good. No, clearly it is all for the good of the globalists and damn everyone else. Only socialism can lead to globalism. It explains why the world elite are socialist in their politics. It is because they are globalists and their intention is to rob every individual of as many of their rights and as much of their money as they possibly can. They do this with the aid of socialist policies passed by governments of all stripes, often believing they are doing something good for their own society. But remember, if you empower the society, you disempower the individual, no matter how good your intentions.

"The road to hell is paved with good intentions"

Proverb

Where does the government fit into an individualist society? Individualists believe that the government is a necessary evil. They believe that the government works for the people and is there to protect the people and make sure they are not defrauded. To achieve this, the state should be responsible for national defence, the police force and a fair and accessible judicial system. This means that the state should be just large enough to achieve these modest objectives and no larger. This is the belief system of a Libertarian, which is about as far as you can get from being a Socialist. Unfortunately, libertarianism has a few inherent flaws and as a societal model is no more viable that socialism. In a libertarian society, you are free to do whatever you want as long as you don't take anyone else's rights away from them. To achieve this ultimate goal, there are two basic tenets to live by. The first is the policy of non-aggression. This means that you are not to initiate aggression against another person, but if aggressed against, you have the right to defend yourself. The second basic tenet is the respect for property rights. If something is mine, my house, my words, my crops, my money, my labour, my time, no one has the right to take any of it without my permission. Most libertarians are decent people and contribute towards their local communities in the form of volunteering their time, labour, money or produce to help those in their communities that are unable to look after themselves. However, in a libertarian society, you must have something to give in order to get. If you cannot work or have no talents, you are severely disadvantaged. Individualism organizes a Libertarian society to address this basic inequality, the only inequality of outcome that is regulated in an individualist society. Individualist policies written to benefit the individual will always take account of and make allowances for those who are unable to help themselves.

Before we close this chapter, now that we have disassociated capitalism from being the opposite of socialism, I want to point out a few things that are not apparent under the old paradigm, but which start to come into focus a little better. I'm going to make a couple of statements that your first instinct will be to disregard out of hand. I urge you not to do this.

Our central banking system is a feudalist system

Let's look a little more closely at this. In a feudal system you have a few people at the top that own everything, and everyone works for them, even the free people. With our central banking system, a few people own everything and everyone else works for the bank. Even if you don't owe directly to the bank, the money that you do work for was created with debt attached, debt to the central bank. Therefore, your children and grandchildren are in debt to pay for the money supply that was created yesterday and the day before, even though it was created without your permission. This is why one of the things that an individualist society must do is abolish the central banking system and its abhorrent practice of fractional reserve banking. The people are responsible for the wealth creation in a society; therefore, they should also own the money supply. No one else is entitled to create money with debt attached and charge interest on the money used. No one has the right to force you into a debt situation without your permission, let alone without you even knowing about it, which is the current situation in all but a handful of countries around the world.

In our current quasi-socialist societies, people own the means to create the money. However, the banks and the whole banking supersystem have fooled us into thinking that they are the ones who own the means to create the money. I'm going o take a short detour here to explain that I am not talking about the means to print

What is the Problem?

bank notes. That is not creating money, it is printing bank notes. Currently, this is in the domain of the privately-owned central banks but should in fact be under the control of the state. The state should have a programme for gathering up old, damaged and worn out bank notes, destroying them and printing an exact amount of new bank notes to replace the destroyed ones. The state would not need permission from the people to do this as there is no extra money in circulation and therefore the money in people's pockets, bank accounts and pension funds is not affected. However, printing more bank notes above and beyond the replacement of lost or damaged notes should only be done with a mandate from the people. After all, printing "money" with no corresponding increase in the strength of the economy leads to inflation, which in turn devalues the money in the pockets, bank accounts and pension funds of the people. Quantitative Easing is just another phrase for "government sanctioned fraud". If you or I simply printed more money[2], we would be locked up. But when the government ask the privately-owned central banks to do it (having first been asked by the central banks to pass the required legislation) it is considered legitimate. This is a clear socialist policy.

Back to the real creation of money. Individuals create money with their labour or their production. The government has no money of its own. All money is owned by the people. If an individual person wishes to, they can sign away their rights to their ownership of, some or all of their future income of production. In exchange for a "lump sum" of money now. This may be done using some form of Promissory Note such as a loan agreement, a mortgage or a bill of exchange. This is how that works.

Let's assume that you want to buy a house and your current level of production earns you an income at a certain level and your current circumstances dictate that it is likely that your production will continue at this level or better for the foreseeable

---

[2] The equivalent of you or I "printing more money" would be to take out two or more insurance policies covering the same asset or taking out loans for twice as much money as we could afford to repay. As you may be aware, there are laws to stop us as individuals from doing this. However, there are no such laws to prevent the central bank or the government from doing similar things. Governments can ask the central banks to print as much money as they want by issuing "government bonds" with no mandate from the people, even though the people are the ones that will be repaying the debt at the future-inflated price.

future. Let's assume that you have also saved a deposit amount, which a lender often requires so that there is a little equity in the property which they can claim should anything go wrong with your means to repay your "debt". If the lender is satisfied that you meet all of their criteria for that particular arrangement, which will be different for a mortgage or a secured loan or an unsecured loan or an overdraft, etc., they will ask you sign a promissory note or something similar promising to repay from your future production the amount that they are going to lend you. When you sign the document, you have created the money that you wish to use. Your promise to pay a certain amount of money every month, year or over the lifetime of the loan is cold, hard currency. It is as good as cash. Once this is done, the lender sells your promissory note on Wall Street or in The City or elsewhere where promissory notes can be exchanged, and they get you the money you have created. Then they give you the money that you have created and they set themselves up as the collectors of the debt, even though you do not owe that "lender" the money any more. They have already sold your promissory note and it is out in the stock exchanges of the world being traded on every day, stored, transmitted from one person to another, every single day. The money they gave you was your money.

The banking supersystem would love for you to believe that they are lending you their money so that when you repay it, you repay them. This is how the banking system has grown to control the whole world. Government induced debt is set up to pay the central banking system for yesterday's cash flow which was created with debt attached in the form of a promise for the people to repay the debt from future production. When governments get into debt, as they must do under this rigged system, the privately-owned central banking system provides even more money in the form of loans in exchange for even more promises to pay, backed up by even more future production by the people. Private individuals are duped into repaying the central banking system for money that they themselves created with a promise against future earnings. And all of this money and the promissory notes all flow through the central banking system to a few wealthy individuals who own everything. The rest of us then wonder "Where has all the money gone?" The answer is that it is all being sucked up by a few wealthy individuals who have

What is the Problem?

manipulated whole populations and set up a system that most people don't understand and yet most people happily go along with, not realizing that they are selling their children and their grandchildren into debt slavery for the whole of their lives. They either don't realize what they are doing or their government is working on this without a mandate from the people. This why I say that our central banking system is a feudal system. It is anti-socialist just as much as it is anti-individualist.

However, socialist systems are open to manipulation by feudal structures, such as our central banking system, because in the socialist world, only power has any currency and feudal systems are very powerful. You only have to look at other feudal systems such as universities and corporations to see how they can manipulate socialist regimes. Universities are totally symbiotic with the quasi-socialist systems in place in most western democracies, with the universities every year creating millions of good little socialist consumers who don't ever question their programming. They acquire as much money as they can with debt attached, spend it on consumer items that will last just long enough for the warranty to expire before they have to buy the next latest thing to replace it. Work, earn, pay taxes, spend so that they can work, earn, pay taxes and spend. All the time the rich are getting richer and the poor are getting poorer and everyone is saying "Where has all the money gone?" and everyone blaming "capitalism" for the mess.

To round out this chapter fully, I have explained that capitalism is not the opposite of socialism, individualism is. So, what is the opposite of capitalism? The answer is as Karl Marx stated originally, Labour. In our modern society, you have the option of exchanging your labour for money. We call this "working", even though a lot of jobs don't involve any physical labour. If the money we receive in exchange for our labour is enough to pay our bills and keep us from the poor house, we consider that we are "working for our living". However, if we take some of our money and place it in an interest earning bond, or just a bank account that pays interest on the balance, welcome to capitalism, If you employ at least one person where you pay them less than your earn from their labour, you are a capitalist. This is not meant to accuse or upset anyone. It is just to point out that you can be a socialist and also a capitalist. They are not mutually exclusive. Your society can be organized along socialist principles but rely on capitalism to produce the funds in the form of taxation to fund the social programmes. A society doesn't have to be one or the other, it can be both or neither. This point reinforces the assertion that capitalism and socialism are not opposites. However, socialism and individualism are. A policy that empowers the individual also empowers the society, but a policy that empowers society, disempowers the individual. The challenge in an enlightened mind, which you now possess, is to write policies that empower individuals knowing that the society will benefit when the individuals within that society benefit.

Global Warming Myth is a Socialist Construct

This point is going to cause a little consternation to hard and fast global warming enthusiasts. However, put aside any arguments about the scientific validity of the theory of global warming, put aside your fears of "what if the scientists that support this theory are right" and let's look at the effects on our society of believing this myth. Firstly, there is a phrase in criminology that states, when you want to find out who the perpetrator of a crime is, "follow the money". If there is no beneficiary to the crime, then it may well not be an intentional crime. If we apply that to "global warming", it will reveal not only that the whole thing is a lie, but that it is a deliberate lie, set up to drive socialist agendas within our societies. The first lot of money is so called "green taxes". There is no evidence that green taxes are reducing the use of the energy supply to which they are applied. It is just extra taxation. If you look at the figures in your country, you'll see that it is a lot of extra taxes, in some cases as much as 25% additional tax compared to not having green taxes. The second money stream to look at is research grants. Since the early 1990s, if you wanted a grant to study anything, you only had to add the words "to study the effect of global warming on" and then whatever you wanted to study. If you did this, you got grant money. If you were honest and didn't add this to your application, no grant money for you. Therefore, most scientific studies were carried out to prove the latest bunk theory about global warming, otherwise future funding would be in jeopardy, thus creating a self-reinforcing feedback loop. The third money stream affected by this myth is manufacturing. Based on the earlier section about central banking, you can see that banks must have businesses and industries to lend to. These industries must have a certain amount of longevity so that the loans can be

What is the Problem?

secured against future earnings. With the advent of the global warming hysteria, the central banking system found it was able fund the media, universities, film makers and governments to get on board with supporting the myth. This created a rapidly growing marketplace into which their funding could flow. This in turn secured their capital because they had created a strong industry based on a popular and emotive subject. The only thing required was for the majority of people to buy into the myth. This was successfully achieved with Al Gore bastardizing the teachings of his mentor Roger Revelle at the Scripps Institution of Oceanography in San Diego, California, for which he was rewarded with a part-share in a Nobel Prize, all orchestrated by those that stood to gain most, the central banking system. The greatest casualties to this wide-spread myth is damage caused to the planet by there being too little carbon dioxide in the atmosphere and damage to third world countries struggling to shake off the combined effects of lack of sanitation, lack of medicine, lack of water and lack of food, all of which would be helped massively by the distribution of abundant electricity created by the introduction of cheap and clean coal-fired power plants or thorium reactors.

So, what is the problem in short? People don't realize that many of the systems and mechanisms that they interact with on a day to day basis are actually socialist systems, designed to enslave individuals and stifle individualism as a political force. If we don't realize this and do something about it, we will be doomed. The rise of populism in Europe and the USA is a great start into slowing the march of socialism and if not working towards, at least acknowledging that individualism is the answer that we seek to solve many of the problems facing us and working towards a society that values individuals above groups, and people above organizations, corporations or other socialist constructs.

Chapter 3

What is the Solution?

We saw in the previous chapter that the problem is caused by the duality of human nature and that under the influence of Karl Marx and his ideology, we have a distorted view of the importance of society over the importance of you. Over the years, people have postulated that striving for a better society would lead to a better lot in life for the individuals that make up that society. Bring the tribal chieftains, the monarchy, the industrialists, the capitalists to their knees and make them answer to the same laws as everyone else. In fact, make them pay more. Whilst this seems like a worthwhile objective, is it really? It is just another example of mob rule. You cannot enrich society by impoverishing the individual. It is a popular myth, but it is completely unfounded in any type of reality.

Abraham Lincoln once wrote:

- *You cannot bring about prosperity by discouraging thrift.*
- *You cannot strengthen the weak by weakening the strong.*
- *You cannot help little men by tearing down big men.*
- *You cannot lift the wage earner by pulling down the wage payer.*
- *You cannot help the poor by destroying the rich.*
- *You cannot establish sound security on borrowed money.*
- *You cannot further the brotherhood of man by inciting class hatred.*
- *You cannot keep out of trouble by spending more than you earn.*
- *You cannot build character and courage by destroying men's initiative and independence.*
- *You cannot help men permanently by doing for them what they can and should do for themselves.*

These maxims are as true now as when they were written. Contained within them are the seeds of the solution that we seek.

The Opposite of Socialism

If there are three people in a room and the only person that has any money is Dave and everyone in the room votes to take Dave's money and share it out evenly, is that democratic or is that still theft? The correct answer is that it is both. But just because theft is democratic doesn't make it anything other than theft. There is a reason Dave is the only one that has any money, and it's nothing to with Dave exploiting his companions. The other two could have learned to make more money or keep more of the money that they got. No one stopped them. They chose not to. They chose not to take risk, to play it safe, to do other, more comfortable things with their life. The result is that they may have been successful in those other things but not all success leads to money. For example, one might be a successful parent, passing on wisdom to his progeny so that they in turn can lead, happy and fulfilled lives. Or, consider the successful teacher from the last chapter, who earned even greater rewards than money. However, as a teacher, even a successful one, there is a ceiling on how much the job pays. The successful teacher should not then resent the successful entrepreneur who risked their life's savings, worked long hours away from their family, got disappointed by trusting people that eventually let them down, lost valuable assets as markets and regulators changed the playing field on them overnight, again and again. If and when they succeed in their quest for money in the form of financial freedom, who has the right to take even a penny of it from them? No one, that's who.

To encompass this new realization that the enemy is not capitalism, we must rethink the "left" and "right" within our political system. Capitalism cannot be "the right" because it is not a political system and whether a society is largely socialist or largely individualist, they will both support capitalism, one as a way for individuals to create wealth the other as a way for society to create revenue. Therefore, capitalism is not "left" or "right" in political terms. Clearly socialism in all its many forms (Communism, Marxism, Democratic Socialism, Nazi-ism, Fascism, Mao-ism, Stalin-ism) are on the political "left" and clearly Individualism is not a "centrist" ideology (i.e. it is not part socialist and part something else), therefore it must occupy the political "right".

What is the Solution?

The inability of socialism to address the needs of the individual on an implementation level is one of the great mysteries of the Socialist movement. Socialists just shake their heads in disbelief or become violent towards those who refuse to see the world from their perspective. The belief system of the socialist is based on what is "for the greater good" and surely "the greater good" is worth sacrificing a few personal liberties for? Individualists believe not. Personal freedoms are the bedrock of their belief system. Socialists believe that if only individuals would surrender their own needs "for the greater good", they and everyone else would be a lot happier. They can't see that an individualist wants to be left alone to pursue happiness on their own terms, not on someone else's. This is the fundamental difference between socialism on the left and individualism on the right and it is almost irreconcilable.

Referring back to our citizen from chapter 1, who is unavoidably detained by their elderly parent and cannot meet the curfew deadline, what could be done better than arrest them, beat them or execute them, the traditional socialist responses to the situation? There are many things, fortunately. If we adopt an individualist approach to the problem, i.e. to the writing of a set of rules to enforce a 6pm curfew but with the rights and wellbeing of the citizens in mind, we will realize that we can be citizen friendly and won't need to jeopardize the reasons for having the rules in the first place. In other words, the rules serve the people, not the people slavishly serve the rules. So, in this case, we will organize some form of leniency in the rules. Here are just a few examples of a lenient policy for enforcing a 6pm curfew:

- suppose that we want the curfew to start at 7pm, we pronounce that it will start at 6pm. Then, any citizens found on the streets after 6pm but before 7pm can be assisted to get to their home. If they are out after 7pm, then arrest them, beat them and / or execute them. Still not ideal, but a little better.
- in the same scenario, we could organize an escort service where, if you know you are going to be detained after curfew time, you inform the local enforcement service where you are, why you are delayed and to where you want to go (home). The enforcement service can then provide you with an escort to get you home safely. They would be out patrolling the streets anyway,

so it would not be a hardship for them to escort you home. The downside is that you may have to wait several hours for your escort service to arrive. This is a practicality but also a deterrent to anyone from bending the rules lightly.

- again, in the same scenario, we could arrange a system where you can be provided with a "pass", a document sent to your mobile phone or printed that can be presented to the enforcement team, granting you access along the route from your elderly parent to your home. If you are found elsewhere or outside the stated time, then you could be interrogated, etc.

Individual-friendly solutions are easy to find when you start looking for them. We just need to focus more on the individual and less on enforcement of blanket rules that will never be suitable in all circumstances. In fact, that one observation could improve the happiness level of most people by 20 to 30%. We are all fed up being treated like a number when we are the customer or the client and supposedly the recipient of the service to which we are subscribing.

Before we go much further along this road, I want to revisit definitions for the words I am using.

- The current definition of Socialism is "a political and economic theory of social organization which advocates that the means of production, distribution, and exchange should be owned or regulated by the community as a whole". I propose the following definition "a political influence that tends towards policies that benefit the largest possible sector of society" and that is what I mean to in this book when I use the word "socialism".

- The current definition of Individualism is "the habit or principle of being independent and self-reliant". I propose the following definition "a political influence that tends towards respecting and supporting the sovereignty of each and every individual within a society" and that is what I mean in this book when I use the word "individualism".

In a healthy and inclusive society, it is clear that policies are required to address the needs of society and the needs of the individual. Some policies will be heavily entrenched at one end of the spectrum, such as national defence, and some at the

What is the Solution?

other end such as the right to bear arms or the right to abortion. What has torn socialists apart over the years is their failure to recognize the needs of individuals. Everything is about group identity. They stubbornly refuse to accept that any individual with an opposing view may have a valid point. If things don't fit with their socialist agenda, it doesn't get considered, it doesn't even get listened to.

The idea of identifying this duality in policy making is to enable effective policy making. Before a policy is formulated, there is always the question of "Why?". Why do we need this policy? The answer may appear to be apparent, but until it is written down, it is not clear that everyone involved in the process has the same understanding. Part of the answer to that question is another question - "Does this affect society in groups or are we more concerned about the individuals?" This is a more complex question and the answer will be very revealing and very instructive about how to write and, more importantly, how to enforce the resultant policy.

An example of a socialist policy is the Patriot Act. In the USA the Patriot Act was written into law in 2001. In it, citizens gave up many of their rights if they were arrested under this act. Arrestees do not have the right to a telephone call, do not have a right to legal representation, may be held indefinitely whether charged with a crime or not and may even be released without explanation or apology. Clearly, this policy does not have any regard for the individual, it is considered that "the greater good" is more important than the individual's rights. Most people would agree with this policy, until they consider how open a policy like this is to abuse, or when they find themselves on the receiving end of this blunt instrument that is being applied for purposes other than those that were intended, i.e. for illegitimate reasons.

Many policies have been written that are ostensibly to strengthen the rights of the individual. However, many more have been implemented that erode the rights of the individual and strengthen the control of the state over the individual. I believe this has happened partly because policy makers have not realized that the opposite of socialism is individualism. When you empower the state, you disempower the individual. But when you empower the individual, you empower the state. Unless it is a very small and utilitarian state, the state is the enemy of the people, but the people are not the enemy of the state, regardless of how much the state wants to believe that they are.

"When you empower the state, you disempower the individual. But when you empower the individual, you empower the state"

Andy Galloway

The problem with thinking that capitalism is the opposite of socialism is how that affects your policy making. It is possible to write policies that empower the state without taking anything away from capitalism, therefore there are no checks and balances on the reason for or the enforcement of those policies. Of course, capitalism isn't affected at all if individuals can be locked up without reason and stripped of their basic human rights. But Capitalism is not a political ideology, it is the description of the money-making process within a society i.e. someone can have their money go out to work for them rather than they go out to work themselves. Capitalism, like money is not good or bad, it's how you use it. So why do socialists not like capitalism? Capitalism in a socialist society feeds the state, whilst capitalism in an individualist society feeds the people. It's strange because socialists argue against capitalism, yet, when in power politically, they need capitalism to fund their socialist programmes. Then you realize the truth of it, it is not capitalism the socialists hate, it is capitalists. They resent individuals having most of the money, regardless of how honestly it was obtained. They feel they, through the state, should be the controllers of money, even though they have no expertise or skill at acquiring money and a great track record for misusing and abusing money. Don't get me wrong, there are plenty of capitalists who are reprehensible human beings. That is not the fault of capitalism, that is the fault of them being a reprehensible human being. In the blindness of their identity politics, socialists identify a few unworthy capitalists and tar all capitalists with the same brush. This is as morally indefensible as the capitalists that are morally bankrupt.

What is the Solution?

No one would try to sanction the actions of some of the most successful capitalists when what they are doing is inherently, morally wrong. Many of these morally bankrupt capitalists call themselves socialists and democrats, they claim to put "the greater good" ahead of everything else, but their actions speak so loudly I can't hear a word they're saying. Many capitalist's agendas oppress individuals, sometimes within the bounds of the legal system and sometimes not. This is not what capitalism should be about. There is a wonderful passage that states "To whom much is given much shall be expected". This applies as much to money as to any other treasure. A true individualist recognizes that they did not become successful all on their own and they pay the best wages and provide the best job security for their people that it is possible to provide. Socialists believe that all employers should be forced into this position. The problem here is that most people that judge others do so by their own standards. This is a universal truth. Therefore, the socialist understands that if they were the one with the money, they would be far from generous when negotiating their employees' wages. Because they judge you by their standards, they think that you will be the same. They know that this stand is unfair to the employee (and they don't like you because you have money and they don't) but they have the power to mandate a minimum wage or a company profit-share pension or cap your salary to a certain level compared to your lowest paid employees. This is easy for them to do and they take great delight in passing those laws. Given the option, they would take all of your money and use it to fund their corrupt and ineffective socialist programmes.

Why that is such a bad idea will appear again in a future chapter. For now, just realize that intelligent policy making must take into account the needs of the society and the needs of the individual, some policies more towards one end of the spectrum and some policies more towards the other end. This pre-positioning on the spectrum must be determined before the policy is written, it must provide the parameters of why the policy is needed and the resultant policy must be checked against that intended position.

The Opposite of Socialism

This has led me to believe that we need something to fill the gap between socialism and libertarianism. I have called this middle ground "Social Individualism". Here is where it fits into the political spectrum.

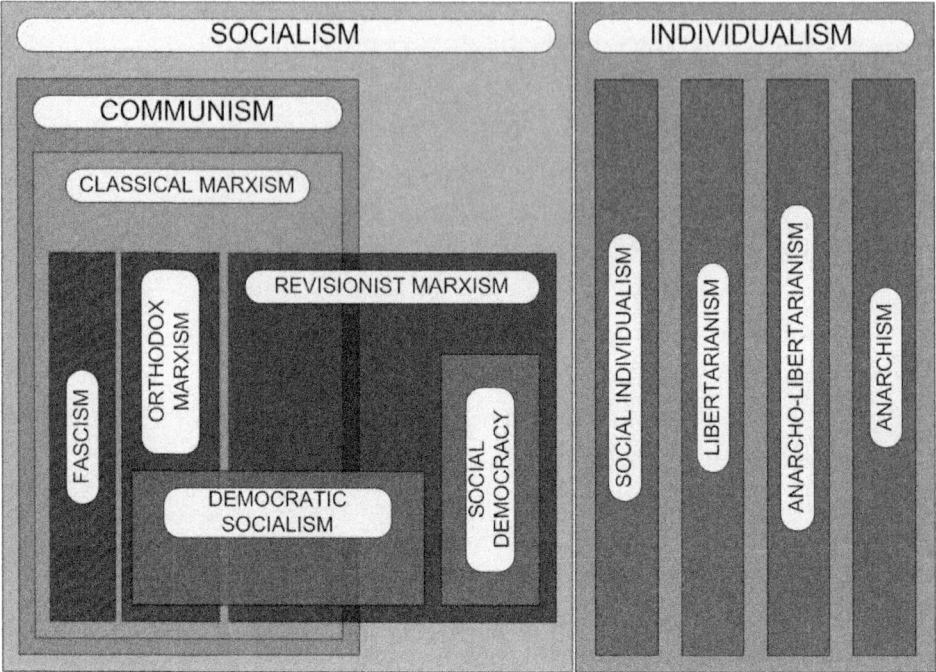

The basic tenets of social individualism are that you do not have the right to initiate aggression against anyone else and your property rights will not be violated. Exceptions to these tenets are permitted, but only insofar as, before initiating such an exception, there is a clearly defined plan outlining why the exception is necessary, how the state intends to redress this so that the exception can be withdrawn and by when will this withdrawal take place. In other words, the business of the society should be so arranged as to eliminate these exceptions as soon as possible after implementing social individualism. Let me give you an example. One of the aims of a Social Individualist state is to generate revenue from the state engaging in "free market" activities. These revenues will be used to pay for the business of running the state. However, until that happens, as a temporary measure,

What is the Solution?

the state must raise revenue by taxing the individuals. The state imposing taxes on the people is a violation of the first principle, imposing taxation is an aggression against the people. You only have to observe what happens if people don't pay their taxes. The violence against them escalates to seizure of property, arrest, incarceration, etc. Therefore, the plan to tax the people to fund government and the state should be reasonable and it should be temporary. There should be a date by which taxation will be reduced or eliminated and there should be a plan for how the state will achieve that. More about this in a later chapter. A fair and reasonable taxation system that does not waste the money raised is based largely upon trust, would be embraced by all Social Individualists. Social Individualists would take great pride in paying their share of a fairly apportioned and responsibly administered taxation system.

Once this term of "Social Individualism" has been coined, there is a sudden realization that it has been there all along. It becomes clear that capitalism is not the opposite of socialism and that capitalism is simply a tool that individuals, groups and whole societies can use to generate wealth. I believe this revelation is the first step towards a more balanced and harmonious society since the confusion introduce by Karl Marx back in the 1840s when he identified capitalism as the great evil, rather than as the tool that some evil men use, but which all people and societies are free to use for their own good or evil purposes. Capitalism, like money or a gun, is neither good nor bad. It is a tool to help the user achieve their goals more effectively. In the case of capitalism, that goal is the creation of wealth. We will see the benefits of combining individualism with capitalism in a future chapter.

Chapter 4

How Does Social Individualism Help?

The reality is that "Social Individualism" has been there all along. Subsequent governments within most western societies have fluctuated slightly on the left of the divide between socialism and individualism. In other words, not many individualist policies are in evidence in western societies and those that are, are under attack from subsequent socialist governments.

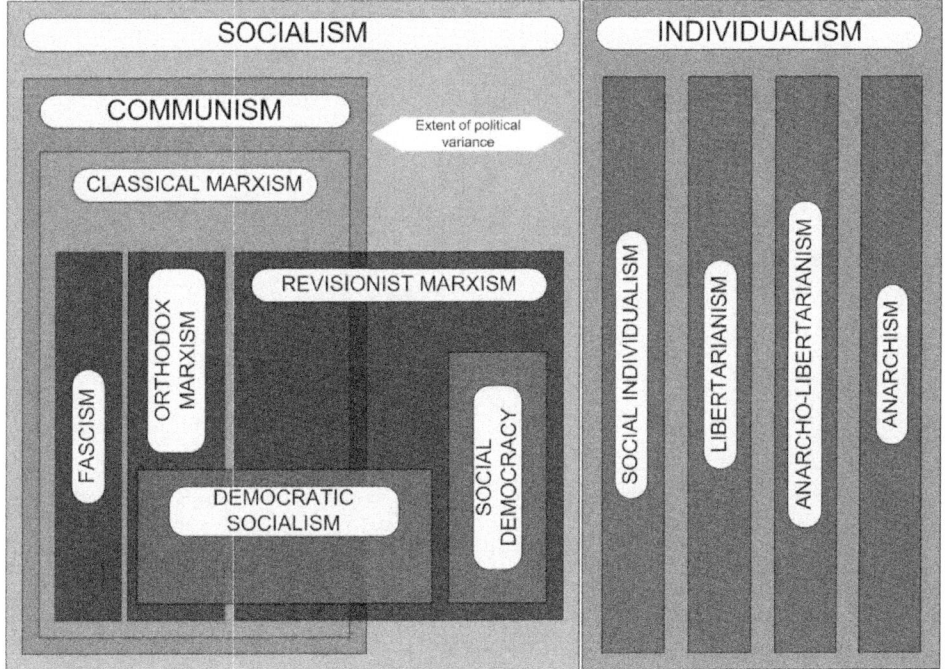

Socialism has had more of an impact on the vast body of legislation in these western countries. You can see that from the fact that socialist legislation rarely if ever gets repealed. Instead, it gets strengthened and more deeply entrenched over time.

The Opposite of Socialism

These are policies such as social healthcare, welfare, taxation, etc. Individualist policies seem to be constantly under attack or made so complicated that they are not worth pursuing. These are things such as gun ownership, business ownership, investments, entrepreneurship, etc.

Would we want a society based on Social Individualism?

To answer that question, we need to consider a few facts about the other political doctrines. Socialism in all its many forms is doomed to failure. Socialists believe the state is everything and all citizens should be subject to the state. This offends almost everyone that has ever been subjugated by a power far larger than they are and which doesn't have their best interests in mind. In a small way we see that when a company gets big enough, they stop answering the phone themselves and have a machine do it. Who honestly likes to have a machine tell them to wait for another person to get around to dealing with them? How degrading is that? Then, when you do speak to a person, they can't really help you unless your problem is in their script. To try to get someone with any sort of decision-making authority to sort something out is almost impossible. If you don't pay, even if the demand is in error, you will subsequently end up in court, with all the trauma that incurs, so you have to persevere trying to talk to someone who has hidden themselves behind a series of gatekeepers. This small illustration points out that none of us, not even socialists, like to be at the mercy of a giant machine that we have no control to influence yet which has control to affect our lives. This is made worse if we are meant to be a customer of the machine because we are paying for our own enslavement. Brilliant!

"As a customer of 'the machine', we are paying for our own enslavement"

Andy Galloway

Social Individualism advocates that the individuals are the most important component of society. It proposes that all rules are written to serve the individuals'

How Does Social Individualism Help?

needs first and foremost. In the above example, the telephone should be answered by a person. The person who will deal with the problem should have the authority to bend the rules or change the process to ensure that the individual gets the fairest or the "correct" result and that person should be readily available to the individual. It may cost more money to hire more staff to answer the telephone calls, so charge a little more for the service or reduce profits slightly to the shareholders. Technology should be implemented to provide a better service for the benefit of the individual, not to increase profits at the expense of the individual.

A society based on Libertarianism has a built-in flaw. It assumes that those who have nothing to give, nothing to trade for their worthiness, will be looked after by friends, family, church, charities, etc. Whilst this is true in some cases, it cannot be left to chance to care for our elderly or impoverished. Although Libertarianism advocates for a small, necessary government to protect the nation and protect rights of the citizens, it is not clear how the disconnect is managed. On the one hand "leave us alone to pursue life, liberty and happiness" and on the other hand making arrangements that citizens are protected, and they don't get defrauded. These two intentions don't meet in the middle. Social Individualism addresses this disconnect by being very open about the rules and regulations that must be passed in order that society can run smoothly. Rules, when they are necessary, must have at their heart the sovereignty of the individuals that will be impacted by the regulations. By addressing this at the policy stage, the rules that are created will be far less complex and will empower the individuals involved.

A society based on Social Individualism will be open and fair. It will be based on a strong sense of citizenship. Citizenship will be the birth right of the children of citizens and will be conferred upon immigrants that have applied for it and have met certain qualifying criteria. In both cases, citizenship will be awarded after a declaration of loyalty to all the other citizens (not to the state) and meeting certain other criteria that the citizenry believe would make for a good citizen. It might be that citizenship is only awarded after a certain proficiency has been obtained with the mother language of the society or it might be that applicants must have a job or run a business before they can become a citizen. Citizenship can also be revoked.

The Opposite of Socialism

For example, whilst incarcerated for particular crimes and for a rehabilitation period once released or within 2 years of citizenship being conferred. Citizens would receive certain benefits such as the ability to claim financial support when in difficulty, rights to medical assistance above and beyond the basic life-saving medical care that would be extended to all residents, rights of equality before the law and protection of property rights.

How has confusion hindered progress?

Not being able to see clearly that capitalism is not the enemy of socialism has led to a huge amount of misunderstanding about the role that capitalism plays in our lives and in our societies. It has also caused confusion amongst socialists. When writing policies to try to control capitalism, they would often find that they are disadvantaging a large number of individuals. This was not the plan when they set out to create the policy in the first place, so what went wrong? They did not have a focus on the basic truth that if you empower society you disempower the individual. They didn't know. Bear in mind that the socialist puts the state at the heart of everything. If you are going to have a welfare programme, it must be run by the state, a social health programme, it must be run by the state, etc. They cannot envisage anything being done to benefit the people except that the state mandates it, funds it and implements it.

The reality of the situation is that you cannot write any rules that don't disadvantage someone. Socialists try to write broad rules to cover large groups whilst individualists don't see the need for rules at all, guiding principles are enough. Socialists create hard and fast rules and, when they don't work as well as anticipated, they amend the rules, repeal and replace the rules, but always with an ever more complicated, ever more draconian set of hard and fast rules that must be applied to everyone. This meets their ideas of "fairness and equality".

Social Individualists recognize that the duality of the human condition must be reflected in the duality of our politics. This means that they try to empower the society and the individual but starting from the other end. When they write a set of rules, first it addresses the needs of the individual and there are a set of contingencies to follow when the rules don't fit any particular individual. They

How Does Social Individualism Help?

believe that if you address the needs of the "mainstream" individual and also the "exceptions to the rule" individuals, that set of rules then covers everyone, which in turn is beneficial for the larger society. Any set of rules should work effectively for 99.9% of people that it impacts, the people administering the service as well as the customers. This approach requires people to be trained in the application of the rules but free to change the rules, within certain guidelines, to achieve the stated objective. It is the outcome that is important, not the slavish box-ticking exercise that passes for state run bureaucracy in most societies. Social individualists realize that the way to an harmonious society is to have harmonious citizens. Socialists believe that everyone should "do as they are told" and everything will be OK. "Being OK" to a socialist means that all of the boxes get ticked on their check list, regardless of whether the desired result was achieved.

If you look back at the history of your society, you will see that all policies either benefit the group more or benefit the individual more, even though there is probably an element of both in every policy. Social individualism dictates that we must be honest in our policy making. We must take into account the idea that when we empower the group, we disempower the individual. For policy writing, we must develop guidelines for declaring the balance of group benefits against individual restrictions in all policies:

- clearly state what the objective of the policy is and who it is to benefit - be honest
- If possible, delegate the implementation of the policy to individuals or social groups such as religious organizations or charities, rather than introducing more state machinery
- make clear and open guidelines about the implementation of the policy and clear and open guidelines about variations and exceptions
- make implementation rules less "restrictive" i.e. trained and competent people can vary the rules when the rules don't achieve the objectives of empowering individuals
- allow people to apply common sense. By all means make them accountable, but make sure the work gets done first, correct any errors later.

The Opposite of Socialism

The running of state business in a social individualist society is based largely on trust. The customers of the state machine are individuals and so are the people working within the state machine. All individuals should be trusted by the state until they prove that they can't be trusted. In that case, individual sanctions or tighter controls may have to be applied to that untrustworthy individual. A state cannot get everything right the first time and it is futile to try, but don't make the system so difficult for everyone based on trying to avoid making mistakes in the first place.

Create the system first and modify it to accommodate the untrustworthy few without penalizing the vast majority that are honest. That is social individualism at work.

Chapter 5

What is the Free Market Economy?

As we prepare for the end of this short work but before proposing conclusions that the author has drawn, bearing in mind that every reader is free to draw their own conclusions from any insights they may have received as a result of reading it, we only need to address one other item. We have declared what capitalism isn't, but we haven't defined what it is. Based upon the redefinitions in earlier chapters we have determined that capitalism is not a political position, both the left and the right on the political spectrum are free to use capitalism to make money.

"Capitalism is not a political position. Therefore, capitalism does not equate to the right wing of politics"

Andy Galloway

When a socialist society "uses" or "allows" capitalism, there are different scenarios that can arise. We will explore the ideal socialist society in more detail in a future chapter. However, for now just realize that the extent to which the state controls capitalism determines the "type" of socialism applied to that society.

At one end of the socialist scale, the "pure" socialism, there is no need for capitalism because there is no need for money and there is no requirement for a state at all. The workers collectively own the means of production, distribution and exchange. In a world where the socialist society has borders with other societies of different political persuasions, there may be a need for a very limited government to oversee interactions with these other societies. The main role would be the defence of the

The Opposite of Socialism

society and ensuring fair trade across the board. This type of socialism does not exist in a human society larger than about 20 highly committed individuals.

Using another flavour of socialism, "communism", the state owns all business and all commerce and therefore it owns all the capitalism. Notice that I said the state owns it rather than the people own it. If the ownership is state mandated then the ownership is de facto by the state. It may be claimed that state ownership is for the good of the people, and that may be the original intention, but that has never been the case any time state owned capitalism has ever been tried. These are the examples that we can point to an declare "that socialism doesn't work". Whilst that is true when referring to this state-owned capitalism form of socialism, this narrow field is not all of "socialism". Additionally, proponents of socialism point to these same examples and declare "true socialism has never been tried" and they too are correct. This form of socialism has not worked and will never work. It is not the sort of socialism that Karl Marx dreamed of or wrote about. For a modern-day socialist to still be working towards this form of socialism after its many, many failures, resulting in the deaths of 170 million people in the 20th Century alone, shows either a complete misunderstanding of what Karl Marx was trying to convey or it indicates that this modern-day socialist has another agenda in mind.

Very often, socialists buy into the Leninist theory that the way to create a socialist state is to take over the state and have the state run the society. Individuals' rights are sacrificed at the altar of fascism or communism. Since the mid-19th Century, the only political doctrine capable of sustaining totalitarianism is a socialist state, where individuals are grist to the mill for the fascist machine.

Another form of socialism, probably the most dangerous of all, is "social democracy". Under this regime, individuals are allowed to retain ownership of their businesses and it is the job of the state to create more and more ways of taking the profits away from the business owners, who are the real beneficiaries of the profits from their businesses. Socialists must take ever more money from those that have earned it and redistribute it for their own ends, for their own gain, to curry their own popularity with the people and to feed their ever-growing state machinery.

What Is the Free Market Economy?

The opposite of the state controlling all business and thereby controlling the economy is "the free market system". This is a slight misnomer because it isn't really free and it isn't really a system. The free market system is what most people mean when they refer to capitalism. It is the application of capitalism by citizens rather than by the state. It is the greatest wealth producing system the world has ever seen or is ever likely to see. It is responsible for raising billions of people out of poverty all over the world and replacing many of the world's largest and most enduring peasant societies with modern "western" cultures. There are a lot of things wrong with westernized societies, particularly in situations where the pre-existing culture has been swamped or thrown away in the hopes of something better. However, when the best parts of the pre-existing cultures are blended with all the benefits of the free-market society, the result can be breath-taking in its beauty, rich in its heritage, clean, safe and secure for its citizens. Less poverty is the serendipitous outcome of the free market economy. More poverty is the undesirable outcome of socialist policies.

Don't confuse the free-market economy with feudalistic structures such as corporations, universities or the central banking system. Yes, they are capitalist systems, but they are not free-market and have no place in an individualist society. Feudal systems love to have the socialists in charge of society. It makes it all the easier for the people to be brainwashed or bullied into being good and obedient consumers, students, account holders and investors.

An individualist society would want to embrace capitalism being utilized by individuals, to enrich themselves and their families by providing goods and services to their fellow citizens in exchange for a mutually agreed amount of money. It is the most sure-fired route to achieving the individualist's dream of searching for happiness on their own terms. Instead of having to be able to make all of the things that the citizen wants in his pursuit of happiness, he just needs to make the money he needs to exchange for the things that he wants. This is so much easier. In this way, a society that embraces a free-market approach relieves their citizens of the possibility of being exploited. If you want it, buy it. If you don't want it, don't buy it.

The Opposite of Socialism

Within an individualist society is the proviso that citizens are protected from being defrauded. This may be in the form of robust and readily useable consumer legislation or may have recourse to involving the police to enforce a citizen's right to be given exactly what they have paid for. The details are unimportant, but the state in the form of the police, courts, judges, etc. only needs to get involved when citizens don't agree on the terms of the contract between them.

There is little more to say about the free-market system. It is what most people mean when they use the word "capitalism". But it is not capitalism that has raised millions of people all over the world out of poverty, but rather the free market. State run capitalism will not produce wealth for the citizens, what it produces is used to feed the state. To create wealth, a society needs two things, a free-market economy and capitalism in the hands of individuals. Additionally, the freer you make the free market, free from regulation and restraint, the faster the economy grows. Over-regulation stifles the free-market economy.

Chapter 6

An Ideal Socialist Society

There are many positions on the socialism spectrum,

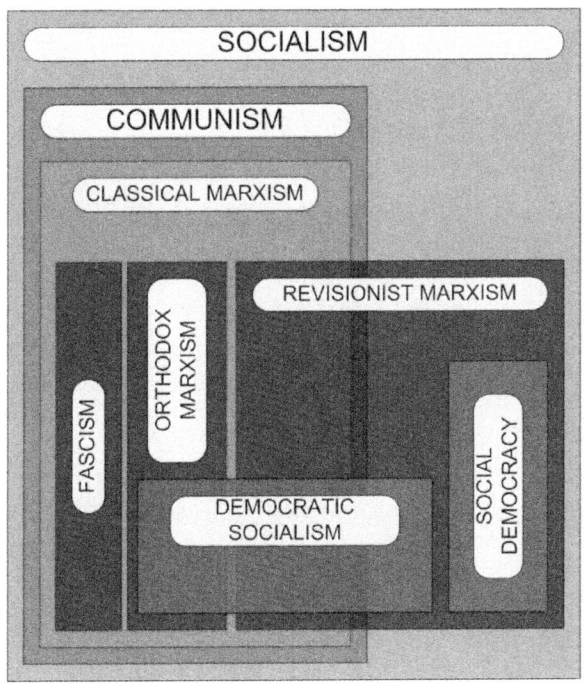

For purposes of this exercise, let us imagine a territory where our ideal socialist society is free from outside influence and external threats. This is a place where the socialist dream can be planted and can grow.

There is a mantra repeated by socialists around the world that "true socialism has never been tried" and that is why the attempts by Stalin, Hitler, Mussolini, Mao, Pol Pot, Che Guevara, et al have failed, and failed spectacularly. Because they haven't

The Opposite of Socialism

tried "true" socialism. This is true, but not in the way that these modern-day socialists mean it. What they mean is that if they had been in the driving seat of Stalin's USSR or Hitler's Nazi party, they would not have succumbed to totalitarianism the way these other guys did. They would have "done it properly". But, without understanding why all of these other attempts fell so far short of Marx's dream, all are doomed to fail and those who decry this the loudest are the ones shortest on understanding.

The basic tenet of socialism is that the means of production, distribution and exchange of the labour is owned by the workers, the proletariat. This sounds idealized and it is. As soon as we start to set up this society, we will see the abandonment of the duality of human nature in favour of something that looks like a good idea. We will see immediately the point at which socialism deviates from its own basic precepts. This then highlight the problem with socialism and, by extension, the problem with socialists.

Imagine a farm with 100 workers. These workers are equal and each has a right to the fruits of their labour. However, there will be some decisions that must be taken collectively. We can't have one farmer growing corn and another farmer raising cows that eat all the corn. Or one farmer wants to take their produce to one market whilst another wants to sign a contract with the local supermarket. There has to be a consensus on certain things, which means there must be compromise on certain things. Under the "majority rules" mandate, which itself is the socialist version of "might is right", the minority give up their ideas of what they want "for the greater good" or for the benefit of the collective. Immediately you have the collective suppressing the individual, even though all individuals in this society are supposed to be equal. This is the first plank in the socialist's plan. Convince the workers that they own their own labour, then ensure "the collective" assumes control over the production, distribution and exchange of the fruits of their labour. That didn't take long. The workers have been subsumed on day one of our ideal socialist society. Now it's all about the collective, which may or may not afford the workers any rights at all with regards to their ownership of the production, distribution and exchange of the fruits of their labour.

An Ideal Socialist Society?

Now imagine a society where everyone, 100% of the population, were productive workers, except one. Let's say that person is the one and only bureaucrat within the whole society. This person represents the state or the government. They are the person that has taken it upon themselves to allocate labour quotas or determine exchange rates or monitor compensation for the labourers or any one of a million other things that a state would normally do in this situation. However, Marx foresaw the fallacy of this situation. That bureaucrat is not a worker, they are not producing anything therefore they do not own any part of the production, distribution or exchange of the goods produced by the labour. Even if you argue that his own work constitutes labour, the labour is not productive. Therefore, even if he does own his labour, it is worthless because his labour is non-productive. However, this non-productive person still needs to be paid or he will starve. Therefore, he is paid out of the proceeds generated by the productive workers. In effect, the maintenance of the state is only achieved by taxation of the workers.

Marx believed that a socialist society would be one with no state and no government. Most socialists get this wrong. Their way to realize the socialist dream is to take over the state then usher in a new age of socialist enlightenment. However, once they take over the state and find out what it's like to wield a little power, they quickly forget that the plan was to create a socialist society. They get "stuck" with a "socialist state", which is a contradiction in terms. Having worked so hard to overthrow the previous incumbent bourgeoisie, they move into that role themselves and decide to protect their position of power without realizing that they themselves have now destroyed their own socialist dream. They see enemies around every corner and mistrust in every word spoken to them because they judge those around them by their own standards, as all who judge are prone to do, and they know that they themselves are untrustworthy, greedy and deceitful. Therefore, everyone around them must be as well, even their own family members.

So, rather than pushing on to dismantle the state and return everyone to productive labour, these erstwhile socialists take over the state and get stuck there, like the little boy pulling faces who gets stuck when the wind changes. Worse, they can't see a way out of this mess because they cannot comprehend true socialism. If all

The Opposite of Socialism

workers own the means of production, distribution and exchange of their labour, what need do they have of leaders, diplomats, bureaucrats, quota directors, exchange rate consultants, managers or supervisors? The answer is, they do not. These roles and tasks are a hangover from feudal societies where the orders of the upper classes were conveyed to the workers through successive tiers of management. This, to make sure the production of the workers was in line with the grand plan, which was only known to and understood by the ruling elite. There is no place in socialism for hierarchies of this type. It's not just that they are unnecessary and redundant, they actually break the system. They are anti-socialist and they cannot exist in a true socialist society. If a manager can tell a worker what to do with his labour, then the worker does not own his labour at all, the manager does.

So, herein lies the rub. Left to their own devices, a group of workers will have a multitude of ideas about what they would like to achieve by the production, distribution and exchange of the fruits of their labour. This would lead to some people being more productive than others and some would not be productive at all. In particular, children, the elderly, the sick and injured and those given non-productive tasks such as educating and caring for the young, sick and elderly. A young and hard-working person will struggle to understand why they should contribute to the upkeep of another person's children and the sick and elderly. This person works twice as hard as his neighbour but his neighbour appears to reap twice as much reward. This is hardly the egalitarian utopia that he signed up for. Also, all of these non-productive tasks require organizing to make sure the society has enough educators, doctors, nurses and carers. This creates even more non-productive roles, which also need organizing. The socialist dream crumbles before it has even started, even if the proponents of such a society get past the stage of perpetuating the state that they inherited, they would have to introduce some sort of state, thereby destroying the very thing they aspired to build.

You see, Marx's vision for a socialist society was more akin to individualism than it is to modern-day socialism. Socialism has degenerated into group identity politics and systems to control the workers. Rather than the workers owning the production, distribution and exchange of the fruits of their labour, modern-day socialists believe

An Ideal Socialist Society?

the state should own the production, distribution and exchange of the fruits of everyone's labour. This is achieved through regulation and taxation. In a true socialist state, there would be no taxation. Who has the right to demand a portion of another person's labour? No one. It is his, he owns it. This disparity between what Marx proposed as socialist society and what modern-day socialists espouse is as different as chalk and cheese. If Karl Marx were reading this book, I believe he would come down firmly in the "individualist" camp and want nothing to do with socialism as described in this book and the variations of socialism that have been tried over the past 160 years. He would be horrified to see what the political "left" have done to his work, creating their post-modern, politically correct, group identity politics, undemocratic, thought-police doctrines.

Modern socialism is concerned with building the state, having the state involved more and more in the lives of the citizens and using the power of the police to enforce compliance with the state. The police should be protecting the citizens, but in a socialist society, it is the police that have become the instrument of oppression for the masses. You see, the "collective" is far more important than the "individual". The only use the individual has is his service to the state. The state offers violence to any citizens that don't bow down to its regulations and laws, even though the citizens had little or nothing to do with the production of those laws and their compliance was not requested. Instead, compliance is mandated and, if not achieved, individuals will have their rights removed from them. Fascism is the belief that only the state has all of the answers and that the state should have all control over citizens' lives. Totalitarianism (which most people call fascism) is the violent suppression of the individuals in service of the state. Only socialism can lead to a totalitarian state. Only socialism can breed fascism. Only socialism can perpetuate Nazi-ism. Unless the state is dismantled and true socialism ushered in, socialism will always end in violence against the citizens, often resulting in millions of murders. There has never been a socialist regime where this did not happen. It is a natural consequence as can be seen from my attempt to set up an ideal socialist society, which attempt, I'm sad to say, has failed.

Chapter 7

An Ideal Individualist Society

Whilst this book is primarily interested in the concept of "Social Individualism", it can be seen from this diagram that individualism is a spectrum. After we look at an ideal individualist society, we will circle back to social individualism later in the chapter.

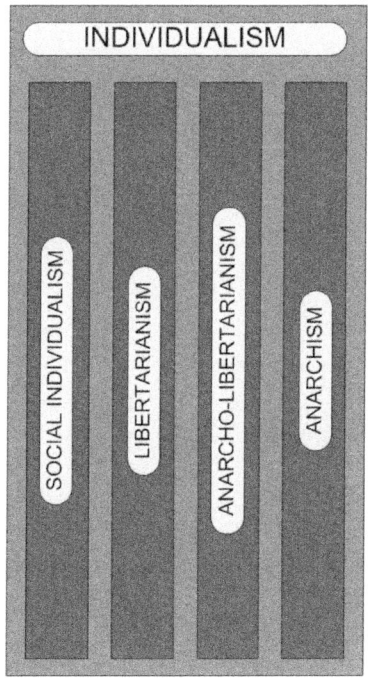

For purposes of this exercise, lets imagine a territory where our ideal individualist society has no need of a state for the purpose of protecting its borders or ensuring fair play between its citizens. It could be that this territory encompasses the whole world and therefore has no borders or it is a single land mass such as Australia, or it

The Opposite of Socialism

is just a hypothetical place where no neighbour ever dreams of invading its borders. The reason we need to stipulate the foregoing is because, by so doing, we can eliminate the need for a state or a government within our perfect individualist society for purposes of protecting the citizenry.

In an individualistic society, there are few rules:
1.   You are not allowed to initiate aggression
2.   You are not allowed to violate another person's property rights

This means that citizens are free from interference from government or the state as long as they don't violate these two rules. However, if you remove rights from someone else, then your rights may be removed from you. For example, if you accidentally kill someone, thereby removing their rights, then you may be incarcerated, thereby removing your rights.

If you earn something or produce something, it is yours. No one has the right to take or use your property without your permission. If they do, you have recourse through the courts for compensation or recompense. This includes your money. The government does not have the right to take your money without your permission. When it does ask for your money, taxes should be raised in a fair and open manner that doesn't discriminate against anyone and it should only be raised for the essential work of the utilitarian state. People who don't drive cars should not pay for roads to be fixed, people who don't send children to school should not pay for those who do and people who don't travel on trains shouldn't pay subsidies to cover those that do. The simplest form of taxation is a simple purchase tax. Every business adds 17% purchase tax to whatever goods or services they provide. That evening, the government removes the 17% from the business bank account of that business and that's it. Tax paid. This simple system can replace all other forms of taxation such as capital gains tax, inheritance tax, income tax, VAT, stamp duty on houses, etc. One simple tax, easy and cheap to administer. Collected daily. No offsets. No clawback. The rich pay more tax because they buy more things, the poor pay less tax because they buy less things and even criminals pay their taxes on time when they spend their ill-gotten gains.

An Ideal Individualist Society?

In an ideal world, the government would charge citizens for the services that they provide and there would be no need to have a taxation system at all. For example, the government could borrow money to build a road. Anyone who wants to use that road pays a toll. The proceeds from the toll road are used to repay the loan and keep the road up to specification with regular maintenance. Only the people using the roads would have to pay for them, which also includes visitors. This is not to be confused with our current situation where the roads were paid for from tax revenue collected previously. In this case, the road is owned by the taxpayer and, therefore, the taxpayers should not have to pay again to use their own road.

This provides the prologue for this chapter. An ideal Social Individualist society would have the following characteristics.

- The state would only be concerned with military defence of the country, a powerful and independent judiciary and strong, all-consuming individual protection laws, supported by a modest police force;
- The state would be in charge of regulating the money supply, abolishing such institutions as the Bank of England, The Federal Reserve, The Bank of Japan et al and destroying the practices of fractional reserve banking and quantitative easing as economic tools;
- The state would raise money by providing a service that the citizens would want to pay for, thereby reducing the taxation burden on the citizens;
- Any additional revenue required, as voted for by the citizens, would be in the form of fair and simple "sales tax" system that affects everyone in society and there is no way of avoiding it;
- All laws and policies of all institutions would be written to empower the individual above and beyond anything else. That institution would naturally be improved by having empowered individuals within it;

One of the great benefits of an individualist society is that socialism in all its many forms become exposed and must be forced to capitulate to the will of the people. For example, most corporations are socialist in nature, that is in the modern sense of the word, not the one that Karl Marx proposed. In the same way, so are most universities. Can you imagine if policies and rules of these great institutions could be

The Opposite of Socialism

overturned by a strong independent judiciary by one individual showing how those policies empower the organization over the individual? It would be a beautiful thing to behold. It would also be quick and easy to do. The corporations would have to think very carefully to ensure that their rules and regulations empower the individual first, whether that is an employee, a customer, a supplier or someone drawing their pension from the company pension fund.

So, in an ideal individualist society, all individuals would be treated as people not commodities. In employment they would all be treated with respect and would earn a rate commensurate with the work they do, not based on age or sex. They would pay no taxation as a result of what they earn or what they are given. They would pay for services that they choose from individuals, corporations or the state and they will pay a small sales tax on everything they buy. There will be strong charity programmes that people will pay to in order to look after the less fortunate in society. They will have a simple health insurance policy, provided by a hospital, that covers everything that they need to get emergency medical treatments. They are free to pay more to have more cover. Professionals such as lawyers and doctors will donate their time and skills to charitable efforts, rather than their money, to provide services to those less fortunate in society.

Individualists also believe fundamentally in Equality of Opportunity. This means that, even though we all start in different places, no one has the right to impede my progress to rise to my own level of satisfaction. If they do so or attempt to do so, they will be removing my rights from me and I will have recourse through the courts to address this. We know that people start in different places. Even identical twins, with the same parents, living in the same house, going to the same schools, having the same friends, and the same opportunities, will take very different paths in life, one twin embracing certain opportunities and the other twin embracing others. Some people start as the children of wealthy parents to end life in a very poor situation, having fallen almost as far as a person can fall. Others can start from very meagre background or "in the gutter" and rise to phenomenal levels of success by every standard you can use to measure. Imagine if they had all been helped by the

An Ideal Individualist Society?

state to achieve the same outcome. I suspect both of them would have led very miserable lives.

Another tenet of an individualist society is a very small state. To get a grasp of this, we have to understand the "Hierarchy of Authority". This shows who is allowed to be in charge of whom within a society. In our Western Democracies, the highest point of the hierarchy is "The Law". It is based on the Judeo-Christian teachings which have at their heart the 10 Commandments as given to Moses by God on Mount Sinai. Whether you believe in God or not, all Western Societies and their many off-shoots have these teachings at their core. This explains why there is such a discrepancy between western culture and the local, native cultures as these political systems were exported around the world during a period of massive colonization of the whole planet by western societies, many European countries. As this political framework was imported elsewhere, there was clearly a conflict with the local religious teachings. In places such as India, Japan, the Islamic countries, indigenous natives in North and South America, Borneo, Africa, etc. Many of these countries didn't believe (and some still don't) that you should not kill, or take someone else's property just because you want it, or that you should look after the elderly and infirm. Many other religious teachings are not based on the 10 Commandments yet, we expect all citizens, regardless of their religious beliefs to live under laws that spring from Judeo-Christian teachings and which are alien to almost everyone else. This clash between cultures, resulting in a lack of "cultural integration" has had a disastrous effect on many countries and the effects are still being felt around the world.

Regardless of where The Law came from, the pinnacle of the hierarchy is The Law. The Law is there to oversee and protect "The Sovereign Man and Woman" . No one is above the law and all are equal within it. Thou shalt not kill does not apply to some and not others. All People have the right to pursue their lives on their terms as long as they don't break The Law, and I'm not talking about "laws" or "statutes" as directed by the state, I'm talking about The Law. In general, breaking The Law deprives another Person of their rights, either violence was initiated against them or their property rights were violated.

The Opposite of Socialism

The next level in the Hierarchy of Authority is "The Constitution". The constitution is the acknowledgement that not everyone can be in charge. That would probably be OK in a commune with about 20 people, but in large groups, we have to organize some to serve the needs of others. These requirements are codified in a Constitution, normally in a message from the People to the "Head of State". The first thing the Head of State does when they first take office is to swear an "Oath of Office". This oath is sworn to the People under the most solemn of pomp and circumstance, a public declaration that the Head of State will uphold the rule of law and protect and serve the People that they have sworn to serve by upholding the Constitution. In the case of a monarch, this oath of office may last a lifetime, in the case of a President, it may be 4 or 8 years. The length of time doesn't matter, the Head of State has sworn to serve, not rule over the people.

The Head of State then puts in place all of the people and machinery needed to carry out democratic governance. This would be in the form of appointing a Prime Minister or a Secretary of State, a cabinet, advisors and the like. They would also ensure there is a system for generating the Instruments of Government, the courts, a judiciary, a police service and Armed Forces. There would also be a system to ensure the People can elect their local representatives. All people appointed or elected to carry out these instruments of government in turn swear a most solemn "Oath of Office". This time, they swear the oath to the Head of State and they also promise to uphold The Law, protect and serve the People and uphold the Constitution.

Now the madness begins because as more and more people are involved in the business of government, the main reason for their existence starts to become vague and many people start "empire building", taking prestige and power from have more people working in their department and controlling bigger and bigger budgets. I'm sure the term "empire building" conjured up everything you need to know about what happens at this level of the Hierarchy. This is the area of the Hierarchy that must be kept to a minimum and the area that has grown out of all proportion over the last 100 years. We find we have government departments and agencies for almost everything these days, from giving financial advice to carrying out personal

An Ideal Individualist Society?

identity checks, from advising businesses on how to do their job better to monitoring the cleanliness of our beaches. The list is extensive and expensive and many of these services could be undertaken by private companies, who would do a better job at a fraction of the price. This is the layer in the hierarchy where the web of government interference into the lives of the People really grows and multiplies. We say that we have made a complicated world in which to live and we have. It is here wherein the problem lies.

Further down the Hierarchy comes "The Legal Person". This is the person to whom all of the laws, statutes and regulation created by government apply. These laws, statutes and regulations are different from The Law, which is at the pinnacle of the Hierarchy. A legal person can be a company, corporation, incorporated partnership, or, and here is the twist that has led to so much confusion over the years, the Sovereign Person is magically replicated at this next level as a Legal person. Let's see if I can explain what is going on here.

The system is being created for the benefit of a particular group of people. I don't like to use labels, but some people refer to this group as the elites or the cartels. We all know to whom I refer when I say that, they are the people who benefit from almost every banking, corporate or government transaction, wherever it happens, anywhere in the world. The money always flows only in one direction. This group can influence the lawmakers to create the laws, statutes and regulations that they want. If they come up against someone with a bit of character and a bit of fight in them, it may take a little longer, but they are playing a long game and they don't mind waiting a few more years to get what they want. So, the laws, statutes and regulations made by the lawmakers without the consent of the People are not valid, they don't apply to the People because the lawmakers are put into office to serve The Law and the People. They cannot produce laws that apply to the Sovereign Person without the consent of every Sovereign Person to whom that law applies.

Now, the idea of making these laws is to "govern" the dealings of the legal persons, ALL legal persons. In order to get the laws to apply to the People, each Person must have a "placeholder" or a "straw man" or a "citizen" representing them at this level. In this case, the straw man is on an equal footing to the incorporated legal persons

The Opposite of Socialism

such as companies and incorporated partnerships. The word "incorporate" literally means "to give body to". It means that you can take an idea of a group of people that form a club or some other organization, go through the magic process of "incorporation" and you end up with a "legal person", an organization that has rights under the law. Now all you need to do is write the laws in such a way as to give the incorpated bodies greater benefits under the law and your coup against the People is complete. The way corporations have greater benefits under the law is because the laws are made so complex. The average citizen cannot understand them and the corporations have everything on their side from the law makers to the judges, through the adoption of judicial guidelines, which are often at variance from the ruling the judge believes is the right one. We hear them say "The law is an ass" and "My hands are tied", but it all means the same thing. Even though you're in the right, you lose.

The switcheroo happened when the Sovereign Person was replicated at the same level as legal people. They were and are represented under the law by a "citizen" rather than in their own right as a Person. Apart from "The Law", these laws and statutes only apply to the legal person, not the Sovereign Person. The Sovereign Person only has to account for themselves when they have broken The Law against another Sovereign Person, not when their legal avatar has broken a statute against another legal person i.e. a corporation. This is the area where Socialism really tears things up because it is where they believe they have control over the Sovereign Person. They do not, they only have control over the legal person, the citizen, the subject of the realm, the strawman, the avatar that was created for just this purpose. Unless a Sovereign Person has broken The Law their rights remain intact. They cannot be forced to do anything against their will. Anything else is against The Law and against the Constitution, both of which the Head of State and all of the instruments of government have sworn to uphold.

In an individualist society, we must believe that the Hierarchy of Authority is absolute. The Head of State and the Instruments of Government "serve on our behalf with our consent and for our benefit", they do not "rule over us". All Sovereign Men and Women are equal before The Law. The concept of Sovereign

An Ideal Individualist Society?

Men and Women having a legal avatar is not a valid one in a true individualist society. For every law passed, it can only apply to a Sovereign Person with their consent not to their legal avatar as a matter of course. This makes law making in an individualist society a very difficult thing to do, to the point that it probably doesn't need to be done at all. If you look at The Law, it is everything we need:

1. Do not initiate violence against another Person
2. Respect the property rights of all other People

This is actually the second half of the "shorthand" version of the 10 Commandments that Jesus taught his disciples and is at variance from the teaching of a lot of other religions and cultures. But in a Judeo-Christian "Western" democracy, it works well. Jesus said "treat others as you want them to treat you". An individualist society would make this its basic tenet and codify it in The Law, the pinnacle of the Hierarchy of Authority.

If no one initiates violence, there will be no violence. However, you have the right to defend yourself if violence is committed against you. Bear in mind that "violence" may be interpreted in many ways. If a government is threatening to lock you up for not paying your taxes, that is violence. If you agree to pay your taxes and then don't, that is a violation of the government's property rights. You have given the government the right to your money, now it is their money, so you must hand it over or you may be locked up. It may seem like a subtle distinction, but it is not, it is fundamental. The point is that one is done without your permission and the other is done with your permission. By demanding taxes without your permission, the government has broken The Law. By giving permission and then not paying, you are the one who has broken The Law.

In a similar way, group identity politics has no place in an individualist society. Every individual is sovereign and all are truly equal before The Law and in fact. In an individualist society there would be no racism or sexism. They are social constructs, developed by group identity politics to divide people instead of uniting them, to make them easy to control by emotional manipulation. All People are equal before The Law. That's it. There is no need of further fragmentation of the identity.

The Opposite of Socialism

The mystery of gender is easily addressed in an individualist society. Sovereign Men and Women are subject to biology, they are either men, women or hermaphrodites. This is determined by their genetic make-up, the configuration of the chromosomes within each cell of their body and is not subject to interpretation. However, one's gender, which belongs to the legal person can be whatever that legal person claims it to be. If you identify the difference between sex and gender as being parallel to the difference between the natural person and the legal avatar, the great mystery of gender simply evaporates. In this way, we can create meaningful rules to cover certain activities where sex is more important than gender. For example, in the world of sports, gender should not be a factor, the determining factor should be sex. If an athlete is biologically male, they should not compete with biological females in certain sports. There are many other examples of activities where people should be divided along biological lines rather than arbitrarily claimed gender identification. Yes, a legal person can choose whatever gender they like, but the sex of a Sovereign Person has a biological identity that no amount of legislation or wishful thinking can change.

We need to be aware that there is the possibility of confusion and what I have described so far is open to abuse by the unscrupulous. Let us suppose that a legal person, say a man, wants to borrow money from another legal person, say a bank. There are regulations governing this transaction and the Sovereign Person cannot at a later stage say that they are not bound by the agreement because the agreement was made with their legal avatar and not them. In that case, give the money back and cancel the agreement. However, it is perfectly legal for a Sovereign Person to dispute that a particular law or regulation that has been imposed upon their legal avatar actually applies to them. The Sovereign Person must give consent to a law or regulation before it can apply to them. However, they cannot be selective in this matter. It is not right that they take all the benefits of a law with none of the consequences. It must be an all or nothing proposition. If you accept the benefits, you have agreed to the terms of the regulation which is, in actuality, your consent. For example, if you think your local authority should not charge you for emptying rubbish bins, so you don't want to pay those taxes, make it clear that this is your wish and then empty your own bins in such a way that you don't inconvenience your neighbours. Don't enjoy the benefits of the service being provided and then refuse to pay because you were not consulted in the applicability to you of that law.

Chapter 8

Individualism vs Socialism

So, before we get into the pros and cons, the point scoring exercise, let's just recap a little.

- Politics as a concept is merely a reflection of our own human nature writ large so that it encompasses our interactions with others
- As such, for people to exist harmoniously and thrive within a society, the politics of that society should reflect the core beliefs of the people within it
- Socialists believe that the collective is everything and people must live to serve the collective
- Individualists believe that the sovereign person is everything and collectives, if required at all, are created to serve the individual

Socialism Causes a Polarity of Ideas

As I look around the world in 2019, I see a massive polarization of ideas. The left-wing, socialist leaning organizations and people are being manipulated by the globalist elite. This is a term that I don't like, but it does sum up the situation quite succinctly. These organizations have had so much money poured into them and have really gotten control of academia, entertainment, the news media and to a large extent, the political structures, that to oppose this onslaught automatically puts one in the minority. It's not that most people are activists, they are not. It's that most people are walking through their lives fast asleep. They are fed the party line so many times per day, per week, per month, per year that eventually, they believe that is the reality. Our schooling system is designed to turn out unquestioning, socialist consumers, that don't cause any trouble for their globalist elite masters. They just get on with their lives of quiet servitude where the best that they can hope for is to live within the confines imposed on them by "society" without it all hurting too much. Our political processes are designed to pass more and more "laws" to

The Opposite of Socialism

hem in our personal freedoms and to sign away our God-given, inalienable rights. The introduction of the Patriot Act in the USA in 2001 was a great example of this. Point to the bogeyman, whether or not he was real makes no difference, and get everyone so scared that they signed up to a piece of legislation that was conveniently already written, ready for just such an occasion. Yet another nail in the coffin of God-given, inalienable rights (see what I did there?)

This steady erosion of our liberties is fuelled and driven by a polarity of ideas. Those under the influence of the propaganda absolutely will not hear a word that dispels the myth that is the party line. These organizations have infiltrated almost every area of our lives through the widespread adoption of social media. The progress of this insidious mind-poison was actually described in George Orwell in his book "1984". The first time I read that book as a teenager, the terror that the idea of such a society induced in me was enough to keep me awake at nights, only overshadowed on the horror-scale by the threat of global nuclear war. How much more the terror now to realize that in 2019 we now live in that society. It is not "like" 1984, it "is" 1984. The author could not have imagined the Internet, so he described the social media interaction used to control the population through media that he was familiar with, interactive television. But it was no less of a mind-control programme than much of what we are encouraged to accept as "normal" on our Internet and in our main stream media.

Internet content and main stream media content that conforms to the party line is sanctioned, promoted, made-viral, re-tweeted, quoted all across the main stream media. Content that flies in the face of the "approved" narrative is shut down, censored, the authors are attacked physically and in every other way. But notice, the "radical" ideas are never disproved scientifically or by gathering contrary data. It is good enough just to attack the person, not the argument. In my opinion, as soon as you have to revert to ad hominem attacks instead of disproving the opinion of the person, you have already lost the argument. Of course, that doesn't help the professor or the businessman who has had his life ruined to realize that his attackers had actually lost the argument when they started attacking him. Their lives are

Individualism vv Socialism

ruined forever and with no proof, no contrary argument, just clever manipulation of the mind-control programme that is social media.

Conversely, an Individualist respects another person's ideas and opinions. They don't have to agree with them, because no one is trying to force them to live by another person's ideas. I am quite happy for you to believe whatever you want, let it affect your life however you want, I'm happy to agree that your opinions are right - for you. Just don't try to force those opinions on me or force your lifestyle choices on me. Socialists believe that they are right, their opinion is the only one and everyone must either believe as they believe or they must be publicly discredited, even if that means destroying their life, so that their opposing view cannot possibly be seen to have any merit at all. This is what causes the polarity of thought in our society, intolerance of other views, ironically by people who advocate that we should all be more tolerant of everyone else. There is a wonderful passage in the Bible that states "as steel sharpens steel, so the wit of one man sharpens another". People who expose their ideas to others and take on board questions and counter arguments either end up abandoning an unworkable theory or they temper and sharpen their ideas to make them stronger and more robust. Socialists generally live in an echo chamber, where the only voices allowed are those of consent and disparate views are shouted down. This is why so many socialists resort to the argument that they must be right because everyone they talk to agrees. Of course, if you disagree, you get censored, your voice is shut out and you are discredited as a person and therefore the worst kind of despicable human being.

This kind of consensus-centric reasoning is a fool's errand in and of itself. Albert Einstein developed the theory of relativity with which we are all familiar and which we know drives our high-tech world and our low-tech universe. There may be a few tweaks or modifications to be had in the future, but as it stands right now, the theory has stood the test of rigorous testing for almost 100 years. However, at the time it was first postulated, this theory flew in the face of conventional wisdom and dispelled the commonly accepted myth about the reality of our universe. Instead of disproving the theory, several scientists wrote a book entitled "A Hundert Autoren gegen Einstein" ("A Hundred Authors Against Einstein"), published in 1931. Einstein was absolutely unfazed by this publication and, when asked what he felt about it by a newspaper reporter simply replied, "If I am wrong, then one would be enough". Thereby dispelling the idea that consensus has any place in scientific rigour. This is the first clue that the climate change hoax is a hoax, because if it were true, someone would be able to point to a temperature chart that shows rising temperatures, we would all be able to see the rising temperatures on the chart and we would all be able to conclude that the chart shows rising temperature. What actually happens is that scientists gather data, manipulate the data to show the results that they want to show i.e. the decline of polar bear populations in Canada. This conclusion, no matter how fallacious, is included in the next scientific "study", which now draws conclusions based on manipulated data and the previous erroneous conclusions and in turn draws even more erroneous conclusions. Therefore, the whole thing snowballs. No one ever stops to look at the temperature record to realize that, actually, the planet is not getting warmer at all.

This bastardization of the scientific process must be recovered. Socialists are not prone to do so. Therefore, individualists must. The scientific process is currently held in full sway by socialist forces. If you are not a "climate scientist" you are not allowed to have a say. This is the shortcut ad hominem attack used by the science community. Scientists are funded by left-leaning government programmes and universities. The only right-leaning studies being done are by large corporations and, as soon as the results are published, the studies are dismissed as "tainted" because they were funded by an oil company or an agricultural conglomerate. It's as if only socialist scientists have any integrity or adhere to the scientific process when, in fact, there is plenty of evidence to the contrary. Socialist scientists almost always "find what they are looking for", they never modify their theory when they discover new facts. They always modify the facts or manipulate the data to protect their precious theory.

The rest of this chapter is devoted to comparisons between a Socialist and an Individualist when considering many different areas where the polarity of ideas and beliefs between them is the most obvious:

Individualism vv Socialism

On the matter of charitable donations, a socialist would say:

"I'll use your money to help those that I deem worthy of help based on the groups that I perceive they belong to. I'll decide how much you give them and when you work harder to make more money, I'll take more from you."

An Individualist would say:

"I'll use my money to help those less fortunate than me. I'll decide who to help and how much help I can give them. If I want to give more, I'll go out and earn more money to give them."

On the matter of entitlement, a Socialist believes:

"I am entitled any own anything that anyone else owns, even if I have to put myself in a position of power over someone to take their things away from them. Because I am part of a particular group, I am entitled to everything that other people in the same group are entitled to."

An Individualist believes:

"I am only entitled to benefit from things that I already own and the things I can earn. An individualist respects your things and your right to own them. They don't want to take your things away."

On the matter of hate speech, a Socialist believes:

Anything they don't want to hear is hate speech that is speech, motivated by hatred for them or a particular group, specifically intended to cause discomfort. This hatred and any speech associated with that hatred is a violence against the subject of the hatred and therefore a crime.

An Individualist believes:

There is no such thing as "hate crime". People have the right to hate others and they have the right to talk about their hatred of others. They do not have the right to initiate violence against another person or to incite others to commit violence on their behalf. "Hate speech" is not a crime because you have the right to hate and you have the right to speech. If your speech incites violence, it should be termed "violent speech" and this should be a crime. Similarly, there is no "hate crime". If you commit a violence, regardless of the motive, you have committed a crime. Therefore, the correct term for this act is "violent crime". The term "hate crime" is a deliberate attempt to confuse people and obfuscate people's ability to understand the reality of the left weaponizing violent speech and violent crime against those that they consider to be "hateful".

A Socialist believes that:

Ad hominem attacks, slander, the threat of violence or actual violence is OK as long as they are used to defend their own beliefs. However, no one with an opposing view is to use any defamatory language or denigratory terms, no matter how slight. Offence is caused by the speaker.

An Individualist believes:

Everyone has the right to say what they want as long as by saying that thing they are not inciting violence. If people don't want to hear, they have the right not to listen. If others choose to hear and chose to become offended that is their right. Offence is in the ear of the listener.

A Socialist believes:

Anyone who doesn't believe every word the government or the state tells them is a conspiracy theorist and should automatically be disbelieved, shouted down, belittled and possibly have their life destroyed.

An Individualist believes:

Anyone who does believe whatever they hear without question is a fool. There is a reason that we have a word for "conspiracy" and that is because they have existed in the past, do exist in the present and will continue to exist in the future. To deny this self-evident truth and to believe the government's story requires massive data deletion by hordes of unthinking sheep

---

Individualism vv Socialism

A Socialist believes:

Regardless of where they started, how hard they were prepared to work, what life choices they made, everyone is entitled to an equal share of the wealth created in a society. This is more important when considering minorities and "disadvantaged" groups. Promotion is determined by quotas.

An Individualist believes:

Regardless of where they started, everyone has an equal opportunity to work hard and become as successful as they choose. There are no minorities or disadvantaged groups. Those who work hardest get the greatest rewards. Promotion is awarded to the most capable candidate.

Chapter 9

Conclusion

I was intrigued to realize that, in the earlier chapter about an ideal socialist society, I could not make an ideal socialist society work, even on paper. It was my intention to do so, expecting that I would end up realizing the ridiculousness of the extremes to which a society needs to go in order to remain faithful to socialist principles. I was intrigued to realize that I could not make a society that worked starting from and staying true to socialist principles.

We may also consider the relationship between "Nationalism" and individualism. Nationalism is simply the identification with one's nation and support for its interests. This can occur in a socialist nation as well as in an individualist nation. Therefore, there is not really a relationship between either socialism or individualism and nationalism. However, nationalism does impact a socialist society differently than it impacts an individualist society.

A socialist society may well be constrained within the borders of its own nation and, ostensibly at least, the society would want the interests of its own nation to be foremost in the thoughts and actions of its leaders. However, socialism is a supra-national doctrine and socialist societies want to spread the good word about socialism far and wide. This may be done by supporting other nations financially, militarily or diplomatically as long as certain socialist ideas are adopted in that country. Over time, the original socialist society can influence other nations towards socialist societies themselves. In other regimes, the original socialist society may force neighbouring nations into a socio-economic bloc through military or economic might. The original society then would have to exert tremendous pressure on the satellite nations to maintain the integrity of the bloc. In these cases, nationalism works against the socialist cooperation between the member nations because all policies in this arrangement will always benefit the original society more than the

The Opposite of Socialism

vassal societies, ironic as it may sound. Therefore, the pressure of nationalism would work to break up the alliance.

In an individualist society, the nation state defines the parameters for the Hierarchy of Authority. The society, in order to operate effectively, must operate within the confines of an area where The Law is paramount and wherein the Head of State has absolute sway to uphold The Law and protect the People. This is often a whole country but can just as easily be a region or a territory. As long as The Law, The People and the remit of the Head of State are all contained within the same area, an individualist society will thrive. In this case, nationalism is a great thing because everyone within the society will have a vested interest in doing their bit to support their society. A small example is the plague of litter-droppers. People who feel that the nation belongs to them would no sooner drop litter in it than they would fly to the moon. Most crime, from minor to major, is as a result of people feeling disenfranchised, i.e. separate from their nation and their society. They feel they have to grab whatever they want in whatever way they can. This is often by illicit means because they see no other way of achieving what they want. They feel that life is unfair and no matter how hard they work, they could easily end up with no rewards for their effort. This is the hallmark of a socialist society and, unfortunately, it is the reality of almost all western societies. These societies have the power to create a fairer system, but choose not to because they are following a doctrine started in 1840s Europe that was based on a false assumption that has persisted and become ever more twisted in the last 180 years.

So, what conclusions can we draw from the preceding discussions?
- Capitalism is not the opposite of socialism.
- Socialism is the opposite of individualism.
- Globalism is the opposite of individualism.
- Free-market economies produce wealth
- Free-market economies destroy poverty
- Socialist capitalism produces poverty

Therefore, in at least one sense, socialism and globalism are the same. Globalism and socialism are both the enemy of individualism.

Conclusion

Globalism uses capitalism, extortion, fearmongering, blackmail, lying, cheating and stealing to achieve their objectives of amassing more and more power and exercising ever tighter control over the global masses. Socialism does the same.

Globalism is the enemy of mankind. It manufactures enemies for the people to oppose collectively and, whilst everyone is looking one way, the globalists are stealing more power and money and exerting more control over the masses. No one is watching what is going on. Examples of this include:

- The climate crisis hoax
- Recessions and depressions
- Wars
- Organized terror events i.e. 9/11, 7/7, mass shootings, etc
- Public health issues and outbreaks
- Riots and violent protests

Another conclusion is that the reason socialism has gained such a foothold in all western democracies is that people were unaware that socialism is the opposite of individualism. If they were aware, many of the longstanding socialist policies would not have stood as long as they have. They would have been overhauled a long time ago to empower the individual, not to empower the state. Examples of this include welfare, healthcare, policing, judicial process, tax collection or in fact, any interaction with any government department at any time. In many of these institutions, the people that work there feel that they are just gearwheels within a machine and that they are powerless to do anything except line people up as fodder for the machine.

By way of an example, imagine a truly individualist society where a man has just left his job and needs to get money from the welfare system to pay his rent and feed his family for a few weeks until he gets another job. Under legislation passed earlier to protect the individual, the employer would be legally obligated to continue to pay him until providing him with the correct documentation. The man would turn up at the benefits office with his letter of termination, P45 or whatever official document he was given by his employer. The benefits office helps the man complete a few simple forms and asks him how long he expects it will take him to find a new job, does he need any help with that task, etc? Then they make sure that the correct amount of money is set up to get to his bank account on the right day for as long as has been agreed. The worker at that department has the authority to make decisions that will prevent the man from getting into financial difficulties, within certain guidelines. For example, they may not be able to authorize these payments for a duration of more than 3 months or they may only be able to follow this process twice in a 5-year period. If more help is required, then an in-depth investigation into the person's marketability and willingness to work may need to be undertaken. Perhaps he requires further skills or even be encouraged away from an overcrowded or failing industry into a more up and coming one. There should certainly be no drama about providing a person with the money they need to avoid financial difficulties at the time they need it, not weeks after they have been evicted for non-payment of the rent.

Persistent or long-term unemployed people should be turned into productive workers on behalf of society. There are so many jobs that need doing that long-term unemployed people could do. They could be encouraged to be productive members of society. One way could be to reduce welfare payments over a period of time. Another could be to make the continued payment of the benefits contingent upon working for the state for a set number of hours per week. I'm sure that most reasonable people could come up with a list of 50 different jobs that could be undertaken by recipients of benefits payments with either little or no training. In this way, society, i.e. all of the individuals that make up the society, can benefit from the work undertaken and the recipients of benefits payments can develop some pride in themselves for the fact that they are contributing to society in exchange for the money that they receive.

The final conclusion is that with the insights in this book, most western societies can decide to make the real decision of whether they want to continue to evolve as a closet socialist society or do they want to recognize the damage that has done and would continue to do and set out deliberately to become an individualist society. In this case, they would need to review almost every piece of legislation and re-write it so that the individual is empowered above the state. This would mean scrapping

Conclusion

most statutes and regulations as they are anti-individualist or no longer required. Accept that they are simply mechanisms whereby the state can insert itself into the lives of the people. All in the name of the greater good but in reality, to exert more control over the population, which is a hallmark of a socialist state.

Training would need to be given to leaders within central and local governments and within corporations of all types, to learn how to write policies that empower individuals. Laws would need to be passed that strongly support individual property rights and police forces would need to be retrained along these lines. The individual is not above the law, no individual is above the law, but no person is allowed to initiate violence on another person, even if they are breaching regulations and breaking statutes, unless they are breaking The Law. Judicial process and oversight would need to be overhauled to ensure the Person is treated as the sovereign individual that they are until such time as it is proved that they have broken The Law.

As a race, we have overcome so many of the obstacles that nature has thrown at us. In the early days of our time on this planet, predators, pestilence, plague, drought, floods and so many other things that used to threaten huge populations. We are living in a time of great abundance and with a little application the whole world could be lifted out of poverty, made possible by the ingenuity of the species collectively. However, we are struggling to get out of the mire and we are being held on the very brink of freedom by socialist ideas and socialist systems that are already in place. Whole continents are being held in poverty due to socialist dogma and the mobilization of socialist propaganda. To move into the great abundance that will allow the human race to really thrive, culminating in the inevitable spreading of our lifeform to other planets and other star systems, we need to identify what individualism is, learn how to build societies that support individuals and actually create societies that will last many millennia into a prosperous and peaceful future. I commend Social Individualism as the societal structure that will assist humankind to achieve these goals.

Printed in Great Britain
by Amazon